Patients' rights, responsibilities and the nurse, second edition

by
Bridgit Dimond MA, LLB, DSA, AHSM
Emeritus Professor of the University of Glamorgan

Quay
Books

Quay Books Division, Mark Allen Publishing Ltd
Jesses Farm, Snow Hill, Dinton, Wiltshire, SP3 5HN

© Bridgit Dimond 1999
Reprinted 2001

British Library Cataloguing-in-Publication Data
A catalogue record is available for this book

ISBN 1 85642 139 2

Reprinted in the UK by IBT Global, London

Contents

Acknowledgements

The original edition of this book was developed from the inaugural lecture given at the Polytechnic of Wales (now the University of Glamorgan) on 24 February 1992. The author thanks the many colleagues who assisted in the preparation of the lecture and this book. Special thanks are due to June Lewes, Gillian Reeve, Bette Griffiths, Tessa Shellens and Jim Richardson for their invaluable assistance and suggestions.

Introduction

Patients' rights

The term patient's rights appears to be of recent origin. Certainly the rights language associated with Thomas Paine and the social contract of Rousseau and John Locke were not concerned with the human being in sickness. Only recently has there been concern with the rights of the patient in relation to health care.

Codes of professional conduct have of course had a much longer history, for example the Hippocratic oath, but these have been couched in the language of the duties of the professional rather than in that of the rights of the patient.

Until the present time we have not in this country had a Bill of Rights. There has therefore been no document which sets out fundamental inalienable rights which the judges look to in deciding cases brought before them. Instead, in the past, if a person claimed that the law recognised a particular right he had to point to an Act of Parliament (ie. a right given by Statute) or to a previous case where such a right was recognised by the judges in order to support his claim. If this could not be established there was a likelihood that the claim would be lost. This is, however, about to change.

This country was a signatory of the European Convention of Human Rights (see *Appendix I)* in 1951. Until the present time, the Government has never accepted that the clauses in the Convention could be directly recognised by British judges. Any claimant in the past has had to take the case as far as he could within the legal systems of the United Kingdom and if he then failed he could go to Strasbourg where the European Court of Human Rights sits. If he won his case, there were no direct means of its findings being enforced in this country. All this could take an extremely long time — perhaps six to seven years within our own judicial system and then a further eight years in Strasbourg. This can hardly be seen to meet the needs of justice. In 1997 the Government published its Human Rights Bill, which became the Human

Rights Act 1998. This will have the effect of recognising the main clauses of the European Convention of Human Rights as being directly binding on the courts in this country. The implications of this major change are considered in *Chapter 7*.

Why the preoccupation with the rights of the patient?

The recent emphasis on patients' rights can be seen to stem from two main sources. These are shown in *Figure introduction 1*.

Figure introduction 1: Changing attitudes to health care

1. Rise in expectations
    - advances in medical knowledge
    - higher standards of living
    - increased familiarity with health care and carers
2. Concern at harmful effects of medical care

Raised expectations

As medical technology has advanced it is inevitable that this advance brings in its wake higher expectations of medicine, hospital care and health professionals. In the nineteenth century hospitals were places to avoid. Few would have a certainty of coming out alive. Yet now short stay for acute conditions has become almost part of our pattern of life. The establishment of the National Health Service within the Welfare State has crystallised these expectations in terms of the right to receive treatment without payment at the point of need.

Along with these expectations in relation to professional care, patients also expect higher standards in relation to the physical environment. Choice of menu is now routine. A high standard of furnishings and fittings is demanded. Even though there may still remain some hospitals and wards which reflect conditions of an earlier era, for the most part these are subject to planning proposals for refurbishment or replacement.

It is clear too that in the context of these higher expectations patients are more likely to be prepared to voice their concerns and occasionally their complaints. In 1974 Community Health Councils were established with the function of bringing the consumer's views into the planning and provision of health care. They very quickly took on the role of assisting the patient in bringing and processing complaints. In the same year the office of the Health Service Commissioner (the Ombudsman) was established. The function of this office is to investigate those complaints which the complainant considers still require further investigation even after the health authority has concluded its own investigation. In 1996 a new complaints procedure was implemented following the proposals of the Wilson report 'Being Heard'. The philosophy of the new complaints procedure is to secure, as far as is possible, resolution at local level. If this cannot be obtained, there may be referral to an independent review panel. From this panel there can be an application to the Health Service Commissioner, whose jurisdiction was extended to include matters relating to clinical judgement and family practitioner complaints.

The procedures and organisations are therefore in place to facilitate the handling of complaints. Familiarity with the health scene and its employees perhaps makes it easier for patients to voice their concerns. The NHS is the largest employer in the country: there can be few who do not know someone employed by the NHS or who do not know someone who has been a patient. The preoccupation of the media, particularly television, with both fictional and non-fictional accounts of health care result in raised expectations for patients, and these expectations can be contrasted with the actual service provided. These expectations are then expressed in the language of rights.

Protection against health professionals

The second source of concern with patients' rights is of a very different nature. It stems from the work of such medical sociologists as Illich. He condemned the recent trend of medicalising human problems. Divorce, bereavement, redundancy, retirement, road traffic offences and similar causes of stress are treated as medical incidents resulting in medication being prescribed. At the same time, increasing evidence of the harm and side effects of certain drugs has become available: patients are receiving treatment for the side effects of drugs, and sometimes for the side effects of those drugs prescribed to alleviate the side effects of the original drugs. This harm is known as iatrogenic illness. Patients need to know about such possibilities. They should be given such information before they consent to receiving treatment. Thus, there has been an emphasis on the protection of the patient and the patient's rights in relation to consent and to access to information.

This development has occurred over recent years and can be clearly seen in a comparison of the Mental Health Act of 1959 with that of 1983 (see *Figure introduction 2*). This latter Act shows a much stronger emphasis on the rights of the patient in terms of the information the patient should be given. Part 4 of the 1983 Act covers the provisions to be followed in the giving of treatment to detained patients: if the patient is either incapable of giving consent or refuses to give consent, then treatment can be given only under clearly defined rules.

Figure introduction 2: Comparison of the Mental Health Acts of 1959 and 1983

1959 Act	1983 Act
1. Limited access to Mental Health Review Tribunal.	1. Increased access to Mental Health Review Tribunals and automatic referral by managers.
2. No regulations covering compulsory treatment.	2. Part IV contains detailed provisions covering compulsory treatment.
3. No statutory watchdog set up.	3. Mental Health Act Commission established.

It is interesting to note that new developments in medical technology are accompanied on the one hand by claims of entitlement and on the other by demands to protect those who may directly or indirectly suffer as a consequence: resuscitative medical technology has raised the issue of the right of patients to receive it as well as the right to die; *in vitro* fertilisation and related techniques have juxtaposed the claims of infertile couples with those of the embryo; in abortion the rights of the mother to have an abortion are balanced against the rights of the foetus; in genetic engineering the rights of the congenitally disabled are contrasted with the concerns of those who seek to ban such work as being a slippery slope to a 'Brave New World'.

What do we mean by rights?

Authors on the principles of ethics have defined rights as:

'In the tradition of liberal individualism, the language of rights has sometimes served as a means to oppose the status quo, to assert claims that demand recognition and respect and to force social reforms.'

They define legal rights as 'claims that are justified by legal principles and rules' and moral rights as 'claims that are justified by moral principles and rules'. A moral right is a morally justified claim or entitlement.

In this book the concern is not to analyse the underlying ethical/moral basis of rights but to take several currently perceived rights which are relevant to the work of the nurse practitioner and to analyse the extent to which they can be enforced by the patient and how they affect the work of the nurse. (While the term nurse is used, it is recognised that this work is also relevant to the health visitor and the midwife.) This is not to say that it is not important to have an understanding of the moral basis upon which rights are based or to appreciate the underlying ethical issues. These raise very important questions. However, there are several books which cover these topics and they are listed in the *References*.

The rights which will be studied are set out in *Figure introduction 3*. They have been chosen because they figure prominently in the charters and the lists of rights published by charities and patients' associations. These organisations consider that if these rights are not yet recognised in law the law should be changed to include them as legally enforceable rights.

Figure introduction 3: Patients' rights

1. A right to health care
2. A right to a reasonable standard of care
3. A right to give consent
4. A right of access to health records
5. A right to confidentiality
6. A right to complain and have complaints dealt with speedily and effectively.

Patients' rights and the practitioner

What is the practitioner's position in relation to those rights which are identified as having legal force? He/she has a professional duty under the code of professional conduct to recognise and protect the rights of the patient. In this sense he/she has an advocacy role in relation to the patient and certainly might be involved in putting the patient's view before other professionals.

Difficulties however arise when there is a conflict between rights and duties. The practitioner has a duty of care to the patient and yet the patient has a right to autonomy; it may be difficult for the practitioner to decide where his/her duty lies if there is an apparent clash. For example, the practitioner might be caring for a person with learning disabilities who has limited capacity to make decisions. The client might have been given money and wish to spend it all on ice-creams and chocolates. The practitioner might decide that that was not in the client's best interests and therefore try to limit the patient's autonomy. This may seem a petty example to take, but it is the same dilemma which exists in the case of deciding whether the patient should be resuscitated in circumstances where the patient has indicated that he/she does not wish it but where the capacity of the patient to make that decision is doubted.

These dilemmas and the practitioner's accountability in relation to them will be considered in relation to each of the rights covered in this book.

There are other forms of accountability, apart from professional, and these, together with the detail of the legal system and procedures and rules, are set out in the author's earlier work.

Responsibilities of the patient

There has been very little concern with the other side of the reciprocal relationship between patient and practitioner. Yet it is important to consider whether there are any enforceable duties which the patient owes to the practitioner. *Chapter 8* will therefore be devoted to a study of this. Again the emphasis will be on the legal basis of the patient's responsibilities. It will be found that while many responsibilities may be considered to exist ethically or morally, few are recognised in law, especially in the National Health Service where there is no contractual relationship between the patient and the service or its practitioners.

Questions and exercises

1. This book is concerned with legal rights. Are you aware of other rights, which could not be enforced but which you consider should exist morally?

2. The concept of rights can be applied to other areas such as employment. Analyse your role as an employee and identify legal rights which you consider you possess as an employee. Can you identify the source of law which gives you these rights?

3. To what extent do you consider the nurse has a role to protect the rights of the patient? Are there others who are better suited to that task?

4. Have you encountered any schemes of patient advocacy? If so, how effective were they in protecting the rights of the patient?

5. Do you think practitioners should consider that the patient has legal responsibilities towards those who care?

1

The right to receive medical assistance and health care

This right must surely be one of the highest priorities in any civilised society. How far is this right enforceable by the patient? How far does our present law recognise this right of the individual and the reciprocal duty upon some person or some organisation to provide it?

Statutory duties

To answer the question we need to go back to the setting up of the National Health Service in 1948. Statutory duties were placed upon the Secretary of State, health authorities, social service authorities and general practitioners and other independent contractors such as dentists and pharmacists to carry out functions in relation to the provision of healthcare. The duties were subsequently re-enacted in the National Health Service Act 1977. The extensive provisions of the Act can be seen in *Figure 1.1*. The National Health Service and Community Care Act 1990 introduced the internal market in health care by creating purchasers and providers and provided for the establishment of group fundholding GP practices which could purchase secondary care services for patients attached to the practice. The White Paper on the NHS[1] recommends the abolition of the internal market and the establishment of GP/primary care consortia to purchase and provide services for patients. Health authorities will be responsible for general oversight of these functions.

The duties under the 1977 Act are comprehensive and extensive. However they are not absolute. Note the words emphasised in *Figure 1.1*. These words give considerable discretion to the Secretary of State and the health authorities.

1   The New NHS: Modern Dependable Command Paper 3807. HMSO 1997

Figure 1.1: Provisions of the National Health Service Act 1977

Section 1(1) It is the Secretary of State's duty to continue the promotion in England and Wales of a comprehensive health service designed to secure improvement:
a. in the physical and mental health of the people of those countries, and
b. in the prevention, diagnosis and treatment of illness, and for the purpose to provide or secure the effective provision of services in accordance with this Act.

Section 3 (1) It is the Secretary of State's duty to provide throughout England and Wales, **to such extent as he considers necessary to meet all reasonable requirements:**[my emphasis]
a. hospital accommodation;
b. other accommodation for the purpose of any service provided under this Act;
c. medical, dental, nursing and ambulance services;
d. such other facilities for the care of expectant and nursing mothers and young children as her considers are appropriate as part of the health service;
e. such facilities for the prevention of illness, the care of persons suffering from illness and the after-care of persons who have suffered from illness as he considers are appropriate as part of the health service;
f. such other services as are required for the diagnosis and treatment of illness.

Attempt to enforce statutory duties

The extent to which the duties are enforceable by a patient came before the courts in 1979. Orthopaedic patients at a hospital in Birmingham who had waited for treatment for periods longer than was medically advisable brought an action against the Secretary of State, the Regional Health Authority and the Area Health Authority. They were seeking a declaration that the defendants were in breach of their duty under section 1 of the National Health Service Act 1977 to continue to promote a comprehensive health service designed to secure improvement in health and the prevention of illness. They also relied upon section 3 arguing that the defendants were in breach of their duties to provide accommodation, facilities and services for those purposes.

The judge however held that it was not for the courts to

direct Parliament as to what funds to make available to the health service and how to allocate them. The Secretary of State's duties under Section 3 to provide services 'to such extent as he considers necessary', gave him discretion as to the disposition of financial resources. The court could only interfere if the Secretary of State acted so as to frustrate the policy of the Act or as no reasonable minister could have acted. No such breach had been shown in the present case. The application was dismissed against all the defendants. The reasoning was confirmed in a later case.

Heart-baby case

Mrs Walker's son required a heart operation and was on the waiting list. A date was fixed for the operation but it was postponed by the Birmingham Health Authority. She applied to the court for a judicial review of the decision by the health authority. The High Court judge refused her application. She appealed to the Court of Appeal who upheld the earlier decision. The court held that it was not for the court to substitute its own judgement for that of those responsible for the allocation of resources. It would only interfere if there had been a failure to allocate funds in a way which was unreasonable or where there had been breaches of public duty.

The refusal to grant Mrs Walker's application is understandable. Resources are finite; demand for health care infinite.

The case of Jamie B

The issue of the right of a patient to require a health authority to purchase care received considerable media attention in the tragic case of Jamie B in 1995.[2]

Jamie, aged 10 years at the time of the hearing, was suffering leukaemia and had been treated with chemotherapy and a bone marrow transplant. Following a relapse in January 1995, her father applied for funding for further treatment to be carried out. The chance of success of chemotherapy followed by a second bone marrow transplant was considered to be between 10 and 20%. Costs of the drug and transplant were estimated to be about £15,000 and £60,000 respectively.

---

2 R. Cambridge District Health Authority, ex parte B Court of Appeal. *R. v. Cambridge* HA 2 All ER 129 ex parte B

In the High Court, the judge criticised the decision of the health authority not to fund the proposed treatment, but did not issue an order requiring the authority to provide the treatment. The Court of Appeal upheld the health authority's appeal, considering the judge's criticisms to be misguided. It supported the refusal of the health authority to fund the proposed treatment on the grounds that the experimental treatment would not be in the best interests of the child and that the expenditure would not be an effective use of its limited resources.

The Court of Appeal's decision is therefore in keeping with earlier decisions of the courts in general not to interfere with decisions made by health authorities in relation to the allocation of resources. (An anonymous donor subsequently provided the funds for Jamie to receive further treatment, and she survived a further year.)

A successful case against failure to provide treatment

In a recent case the High Court ruled against North Derbyshire Health Authority which had refused to fund the purchase of beta-interferon in the treatment of multiple sclerosis[3]. In its press announcement following the decision a spokesperson for the authority stated that the drug had not yet been supported by clear research findings on its effectiveness. The judge found that the health authority had knowingly failed to apply national guidance in a NHS circular and also knew that its own policy amounted to a blanket ban on funding treatment of MS sufferers.

In view of the increasing demand for services and the limited resources, and the difficult decisions which purchasers have to make over the allocation of resources, there are likely to be an increasing number of cases where patients seek the courts' support in ensuring that treatments are made available.

How will this affect the nurse practitioner?

It means that in the unequal equation of demand and supply the nurse practitioner would have a legal duty to ensure that priorities are determined reasonably. There may well be occasions when patients are refused admission because of an

---

3   Michael Horsnell 'Refusal to give MS victim new drug was illegal'. *The Times*, 12 July 1997

absence of resources. The practitioner should ensure that his/her managers are aware of any deficiencies in resources and that shortages are constantly monitored. Such shortages do not provide a defence for negligence or professional misconduct on the practitioner's part. (As will be seen in the next section the patient is entitled to receive the appropriate standard of care.) However, if the priorities are reasonably determined the patient could not bring a successful action against the nurse or theauthority.

The case of Baby J

A recent case has shone a new light on this issue. The doctors responsible for the care of a severely brain damaged baby refused to put him on a ventilator. The baby (known as Baby J) had suffered severe injuries in an accident at home when eight weeks old. At the time of the court hearing he was 16 months and was being cared for by foster parents. He had become blind, was paralysed, suffered from epilepsy and had to be fed by a tube. The doctors considered that placing him on a ventilator would cause him additional distress and pain. His mother brought an action requiring the doctors to place him on a ventilator. She won the case in the High Court but the Court of Appeal set aside the order and stated that it would not order the doctors to perform any particular treatment if what the doctors were doing was in the best interests of the patient.

A contrasting situation

In contrast, in the case of Re T[4] the Court of Appeal refused to overrule the parents' refusal to agree to a liver transplant for their three year old child, in spite of the medical prognosis that it had a good chance of success, but that without it the child would not survive. The Court of Appeal held that it was not in the best interests of the child for the court to declare that the operation should proceed, particularly as the parents lived outside this country.

The practitioner's input into this debate

It is often the case that nurses, by their constant contact with the patient and the family, have a very detailed knowledge of

---

4   Re T (a minor) (wardship: medical treatment) [1997] 1 All ER 906

the patient which the doctor does not necessarily possess. It is therefore vital for the nurse to ensure that he/she contributes to the discussions that relate to prognosis, and ensures that the views of parents are made known.

Exceptions to the lack of an enforceable right to care

In general it is clear that patients do not have an enforceable right of action to ensure that treatment and care are carried out.

There are however two areas where failure to provide a service may be actionable; not actionable for breach of a statutory duty but as a result of harm occurring through negligence.

A. Emergency services

If an ambulance fails to arrive as a result of a message being lost or of some other negligence by the ambulance service, and as a result of that negligence additional harm is caused to the patient, the patient or his representative could sue in the civil courts for compensation arising from that negligence. This area is discussed in more detail in the next section. Similarly, if a patient in the accident and emergency department is not examined properly, or X-rays are not taken or read properly, or an inadequate diagnosis or treatment is given, and if the patient suffers harm as a result, then a civil action might also lie. In this way the duty of care is enforced.

B. General practitioner services

The new contracts define very clearly the patients for whom GPs are responsible, including those patients not on his list but for whom he might have responsibility in an emergency. If a GP is asked to visit a patient and unreasonably fails to attend, and the patient suffers harm as a result, the patient or his representative can sue in the civil courts for compensation arising from the GP's actions or omissions. The patient has to prove negligence by the GP. It could be that the judgement made by the GP that a visit was not required was entirely appropriate in all the circumstances.

Alternatively, the patient can use the statutory complaint system and complain to the health authority. Local resolution of the complaint is the preferred option; all general practices are required to have a practice complaints procedure. If the complainant remains dissatisfied, the non-executive director of the health authority who acts as the convenor of complaints can, after consulting independent lay and medical advisers, decide whether an independent review panel is appropriate to investigate the complaint.

It should be noticed that in both these areas the patient cannot enforce action by the practitioner or service. He can only complain after the harm has been caused. If a general practitioner ceases to undertake NHS work, or for some other reason asks for patients to be removed from his list, it is the duty of the health authority to find each patient a general practitioner. In the event of there being no GP in the locality prepared to take a particular patient on to his list, the health authority has the power to require the GP to take the patient for three months until the patient is transferred to another GP.

However once the accident and emergency services or the general practitioner have provided all reasonable services and the patient is on a waiting list for either an out-patient appointment or for in-patient care, then the patient takes his chance on the resources becoming available and, as the cases already discussed have shown, has no enforceable absolute right to health care.

Balancing supply and demand

The QALY concept

Health economists have attempted to deal with the unequal equation of demand and supply by the introduction of the concept of QALY — quality adjusted life years. Researchers have determined the value of changes in health by asking health professionals and the general public to make assessments of this value. The assessments sought may be direct, for example, asking people to rate health status on some sort of scale (like a thermometer) or indirect, via people's preference for trading off health changes against other things. Such trade-offs include risk of death (known as 'the standard gamble') or reduction in life expectancy (known as the 'time trade off'). QALYs have been used to illustrate where further investment could be most effective or where reduced investment would be less disruptive. QALYs have been attacked both in relation to how they have been devised and also in relation to the whole approach.

The Oregon scheme

An example of the difficulties of putting QALY thinking into practice was shown by the Oregon scheme and the media publicity given to it. The scheme was based on an explicit recognition that resources available to those eligible for state care were inadequate to meet all health needs and that some form of prioritising was therefore necessary. A formula was developed to determine the priority of each of over 700 procedures on the basis of:

1. how much benefit it provided
2. how long that benefit lasted
3. the cost.

A 'Plimsoll line' was drawn and procedures below the line were dropped from those offered by the state on the basis that their high cost could not be justified by their very small (or very short lived) benefits.

Inevitably, vast headlines, such as 'Survival of the fittest' were accompanied by articles claiming that no longer was treatment to be available to everyone who needed it. Instead, health care for the poor in Oregon will depend on a computerised 714 item list of priorities decided by a mathematical formula.

In the United Kingdom, William Waldegrave, the Secretary of State at the time, said that there were no plans to introduce the Oregon project into this country. However, what would be the legality of such a determination of priorities in this country? As we have seen there is no absolute duty on the part of the Secretary of State to provide every possible service as part of the NHS. Section 3 of the 1977 Act allows considerable discretion. It could therefore be argued that for priorities to be determined in a rational way, such as that presented by the QALY concept, would be acceptable in law and would not be a breach of statutory duty.

At present it is clear that although it is accepted that not everyone can be given the treatment they need even though it is scientifically practicable, decisions over who gets what are not always made on the basis of explicit rational decision making. Demand is controlled by:

1. Waiting lists for in-patient and out-patient appointments (however, Patient Charter standards to reduce waiting lists makes this a less effective form of rationing).

2. Shortage of donors for organ transplants.

3. Lack of intensive treatment units/special care baby beds/coronary care places.

4. Failure to staff such places even when there is a demand for them and the facilities exist.

5. Shortage of expertise.

Alternative sources of help

In addition, as long as demand is not met, some will turn to other sources of help, for example do it yourself remedies or alternative medicine or consulting pharmacists. Ann Cartwright, in her review of unmet need in the 1960s, concluded that there was a high proportion of patients who, for one reason or another, were not seeking health care. It is clear too that the middle classes have benefited from and exploited the NHS more than the lower socio-economic groups. The failure to implement the recommendations of the Black Report is an indictment on our health care provision. In a recent survey a similar, if not worse picture, where socio-economic classes 4 to 6 have the worst morbidity and lowest life expectancy, is shown.

Varying local priorities

Furthermore, certain forms of disability, ill health or needs receive varying degrees of action across the country:

1. The availability of abortion depends, even when the legal requirements are satisfied, not only on facilities being available, but on the attitude of gynaecologists, some of whom interpret the Abortion Act 1967 more narrowly than others.

2. Facilities for community care of the mentally ill and handicapped vary widely, with extreme concern being aroused in some areas. The Mencap report shows the wide variety of community services for those with learning disabilities.[5]

---

5   Peter Singh 'Community Care: Britain's other lottery'. Mencap 1995

3. Treatment which might slow down the progress of AIDS is not available everywhere.

4. As new drugs come on to the market there are varying levels of take up by different health authorities. As a result the present government has recommended a national task force to advise on new medicinal products.

It could be argued that, in the light of this irrational, uneven allocation of resources, a concept such as QALY is preferable to the injustices which currently exist. It is clear that the additional pressures caused by the standards set by the Patient's Charter have highlighted the problems (eg. in setting out clearly the waiting lists) without necessarily producing an answer (see *Chapter 7*). Indeed, any success is likely to be met by increased demand since the current shortages and waiting times might conceal the real demand. Patients might not be seeking help at present on the basis that there is no point; however, once waiting times are reduced, such patients may come forward for treatment.

The effects of the internal market

One of the expected effects of the internal market was strengthening of the determination of priorities and the facilitating of rational decision-making. There is evidence that this did indeed start to take place. A survey carried out by the British Medical Association and published in its *News Review* (2 September 1992) showed that out of 20 directors of public health contacted, 18 had started, or were planning, consultation on health care priorities. Half said that their health authority had looked at cutting whole services including *in-vitro* fertilisation or tattoo removal, and a quarter said that their health authority was considering limiting the scope of services by measures which included the imposition of age limits on patients.

However, it is always open to the Secretary of State to remind purchasers of their duty to provide a comprehensive service rather than cut costs by failing to provide certain services (see the debate on family planning services).

The Labour Government has indicated that it wants to ensure that there is a *national* health service and that access to specific health services should not depend on location.

Reproductive medicine

An example of the advent of new treatments bringing in its wake new demands and the assertion of new rights is the field of fertilisation and conception. The Human Fertilisation and Embryology Act 1990 attempted to answer some of the following questions in terms of the legal rights of patients:

1. *Does every woman have a right to receive assistance in conception?*

   As with the other treatments discussed above, there is no absolute right for any person to receive the facilities now available from the licensed clinics within the NHS. Many are available only privately. Even for those who are prepared to pay and are medically suitable there is no absolute right. The 1990 Act and its Code of Practice places a duty upon the clinic to take into account the welfare of the future child. In one case, held before the Act was passed, a patient was refused IVF because she and her husband were not deemed a suitable couple. They had been refused an adoption on the grounds of her criminal record for prostitution. The judge held that the grounds for refusing to allow her to participate in the IVF programme were reasonable.

   This now has statutory endorsement.

2. *Does a single mother have the right to obtain sperm from a donor bank?*

   Yes, there is no law prohibiting the giving of sperm to a single woman but section 13 (5) requires that a licence holder treating a woman must take into account the welfare of any child who may be born as a result of treatment including the need of that child for a father.

3. *Does a woman have the right to make use of her dead husband's banked sperm?*

   This is not prohibited by the Act but the provisions of section 13 (5) would apply; there is no enforceable right but the licensed clinic would have a discretion over whether to permit its use. There is provision that the child born from the dead husband's sperm is not to be regarded as in law the child of the father. The child would therefore have no claim on his estate. In a case brought by Diane Blood, who wished to be inseminated by her dead husband's sperm, Mrs Blood was refused permission by the Human Fertilisation and Embryology Authority because her husband's consent was not given in writing as required by the Act. However, she did win her appeal to the Court of Appeal against the refusal of the authority to permit her to go abroad for insemination with the deceased husband's sperm.

4. *Does a woman have control over her ejected placenta following birth?*

This is not covered by legislation and common law principles would apply. In the past the normal procedure has been to treat the placenta as clinical waste but it has now been seen as having a commercial value in the pharmaceutical industry in the production of immuno-globulin. The Secretary of State gave a written answer in Parliament on 1 July 1992 that the disposal arrangements should meet with the agreement of the patients.

5. *Who owns the frozen embryos of a couple who died?*

Schedule 3 of the Act requires that before embarking on any fertility programme a couple should put in writing what they wish to happen to their eggs, sperm, and/or embryos if they die.

These are only a few of the aspects which arise in relation to rights. The Act sets out a clear framework of rights and responsibilities in the law of fertilisation and embryo research. However it does not ensure that the resources will be provided to permit those who wish to take advantage of these developments in medical technology to do so. Nor does it cover the vast area of genetic screening and its implications, which will have enormous resource significance for the twenty first century.

Questions and exercises

1. It is probable that there will never be sufficient resources to meet all health needs. What priorities would you set? How do you think the equation between supply and demand could be balanced?

2. Are there minimum levels of care to which you consider patients should have a legal right? If so, how would you define them?

3. The allocation of resources and the determination of priorities is part of the duty of care owed to the patient. Identify how these tasks are undertaken in your area of expertise.

4. Mrs Walker was unsuccessful in the case she brought to require treatment to be carried out on her baby with a serious heart problem. Can you envisage any circumstances in which such a case would have succeeded?

5. How do you define the best interests of the patient? Who do you think should determine the best interests: the patient? the relatives? the doctor? the nurse? anyone else?

2

The right to receive reasonable care

In contrast with the right to receive medical treatment and care itself, the right to receive a *reasonable standard* of care has a long established legal history. It derives from a recognition that compensation is payable on proof of a civil wrong (ie. tort).

Principles of negligence

Figure 2.1 sets out the elements which must be established by the person bringing an action for negligence.

Figure 2.1: Elements in an action for negligence

> Negligence in law arises when a duty of care is broken and causes reasonably foreseeable harm.

The test used in the Bolam case[6] has subsequently been applied in numerous personal injury cases throughout the world to ascertain whether the medical and healthcare service provided to the patient was up to the accepted standard.

The standard of care expected is 'the standard of the ordinary skilled man exercising and professing to have that special skill' (McNair, 1957 p.121).

The Bolam case itself was concerned with the standards of care to be given in the administration of electroconvulsive therapy. In 1954 ECT was administered to the plaintiff without any restraint other than a mouth gag, and with no relaxant drugs. The plaintiff sustained severe physical injuries consisting of the dislocation of both hip joints with fractures of the pelvis on each side. In applying the test set by the judge, the jury decided that the defendants were not negligent. Were the same events to occur today there would be

6   *Bolam v. Friern Hospital Management Committee* [1957] 2 All ER 118

prima facie evidence of negligence because of improvements in the standard of care since 1954.

The House of Lords used the Bolam test in the case of Whitehouse v. Jordan[7] making it clear that an error of judgement may or may not be negligence it all depends upon the circumstances.

Different standards

In a more recent case, it has been accepted that different practices can be acceptable, and thus the task of proving negligence has been made more difficult for the patient. In Maynard's case, a consultant physician and a consultant surgeon, while recognising that the most likely diagnosis of the patient's illness was tuberculosis, took the view that Hodgkin's disease, carcinoma and sarcoidosis, were also possibilities. Because Hodgkin's disease was fatal unless remedial steps were taken in its early stages, they decided that, rather than wait several weeks for the result of a sputum test, the operation of mediastinoscopy should be performed to provide a biopsy. This involved some risk of damage to the left laryngeal nerve. Unfortunately this damage occurred, but the biopsy was negative and the patient found to have TB. The House of Lords held that there was room for difference of opinion and practice and 'it was not sufficient to establish negligence for the plaintiff to show that there was a body of competent professional opinion that considered the decision was wrong, if there was also a body of equally competent professional opinion that supported the decision as having been reasonable in the circumstances'.[8]

The patient therefore has to do more than find a doctor who expresses a view that the patient has been the victim of negligence. The patient has to establish that the actions, omissions or words of the doctor are such that no responsible body of medical opinion would support the doctor. If the doctor (or any other health professional defendant) is able to obtain expert evidence that justifies his actions, the judge faced by two conflicting responsible bodies of medical opinion should find against the plaintiff and in favour of the defendant.

---

7   *Whitehouse v. Jordan* [1981] 1 WLR 246 H2
8   *Maynard v. W Midlands Regional Health Authority* HL [1985] 1 All ER 635

Both the Bolam and the Maynard rulings were approved in a recent case where the House of Lords emphasised that the use of such adjectives in the Bolam and the Maynard case as 'responsible', 'reasonable', and 'respectable' showed that the court had to be satisfied that the exponents of the body of opinion relied upon could demonstrate that such opinion had a logical basis.[9]

Establishing appropriate standards

All that has been said of the doctor is also true of the nurse, midwife and health visitor. The Bolam test would be applied to the question as to whether there has been negligence by a practitioner. How are the standards of appropriate nursing care determined? In practice, following an allegation that a practitioner had been negligent, the person bringing the action (the plaintiff) would have to show that the practitioner had failed to follow accepted practice and that this caused the harm. The plaintiff would have to provide expert evidence of what would be regarded as accepted approved practice — possibly a leading authority in the field or a member of a professional association. This evidence could be challenged by an expert representing the practitioner. Both witnesses would give evidence in chief and be cross-examined by the other side and then re-examined on points raised in cross-examination. After the evidence was given it would be the judge who determined the appropriate standard that should have been followed and whether there was evidence of negligence.

Standard setting

It is obviously of considerable help to the practitioner, the patient and the court if the profession has itself set standards of care. However these will not automatically apply if there is substantial reason why in particular circumstances the facts justify an exception to the normally accepted practice. In other words, the existence of an agreed procedure does not remove from the practitioner the duty to use his/her professional judgement and discretion.

---

9 *Bolitho v. City and Hackney Health Authority* [1997] 3WLR 1151

Implications of the scope of professional practice

The UKCC[10] has suggested that the term 'the extended role of the practitioner' is no longer appropriate; there should be a greater emphasis on the defined principles for adjusting the scope of practice rather than on certification and the emphasis on specific tasks. The principles cover the following:

- the interests of the client/patient
- maintaining the practitioner's knowledge, skill and competence
- acknowledging limits of skill
- jeopardising neither standards nor compliance with the Code of Professional Conduct
- recognising direct and personal accountability
- avoiding inappropriate delegation.

If the practitioner acts in areas where he/she lacks skill, knowledge or competence and harm occurs to the patient, the practitioner will be professionally liable and the employer may be vicariously liable for such negligence. The courts are not concerned as to whether a doctor or nurse carries out a particular activity except where there is a statutory provision regulating the position (for example, the Medicines Act 1968 and the Mental Health Act 1983 require specified professionals to undertake certain activities). The court is concerned that the patient receives the appropriate standard of care. It is no defence to a court action of negligence to say that the defendant had not been qualified long or was a nurse rather than a doctor. The patient is entitled to receive the appropriate standard of care and this should be provided by the necessary supervision of those who have less experience.

One of the virtues of the UKCC paper *The Scope of Professional Practice* is that it places responsibility firmly upon the individual practitioner to ensure that he/she is competent before he/she undertakes any activity; this is more important than traditional lines of demarcation between nurse and doctor. In addition, the courts do not accept any concept of team liability in law; it is for each individual team member to ensure that he/she is following accepted approved standards of practice.[11]

10 United Kingdom Central Council for Nursing, Midwifery and Health Visiting, *Scope of Professional Practice* 1992
11 Court of Appeal *Wilsher v. Essex* AHA [1986] 3 All ER 801

Protection of the practitioner

The practitioner is entitled to protection against allegations of negligence, where he/she has acted appropriately in all the circumstances. This may mean a patient receives no compensation for harm. This is because at the heart of our present system of compensation for medical accidents is proof of 'fault'. There must be established culpability by the defendant because he/she has been found to fail the Bolam test.

'The thing speaks for itself'

The plaintiff has the best chance of succeeding if he/she can establish a *res ipsa loquitur* situation, 'the thing speaks for itself':
- amputating the wrong leg
- operating on the wrong patient
- leaving a swab in the operation site
- giving insufficient oxygen or inappropriate gases during an operation.

Such circumstances will result in the defendant being called on to establish that there was no negligence on his/her part. More likely such circumstances may lead to an offer of compensation being made and the dispute will therefore be concentrated on issues relating to quantum — how much compensation — rather than liability itself.

Causation

Proving fault is only the first hurdle for the seeker of compensation. One of the greatest difficulties is establishing causation, since the law of the tort of negligence requires the plaintiff to establish that it was the breach of duty, ie. the negligent act or omission that caused the harm suffered by the plaintiff.

Many recent cases illustrate the difficulty of plaintiffs satisfying this requirement of proving causation.

1. The House of Lords held that it had not been established that an admitted excess of oxygen (caused when the catheter to measure levels was inserted into a vein rather than an artery) had caused the retrolental fibroplasia

suffered by a premature baby and ordered the case to go for retrial on the issue of causation.[12]

2. The mother of a brain damaged baby had not established the causal connection of the whooping cough vaccination to claim compensation.[13]

3. In a well publicised case, parents of a boy who was given a large overdose of penicillin as treatment for his meningitis had not satisfactorily established that it was the overdose of penicillin rather than the meningitis that had caused his deafness and so were unable to obtain compensation for the deafness.[14]

Medical science is at an early stage in terms of our understanding of what causes what. We have little idea of how ECT or the various neuroleptic drugs work. To establish that B was reasonably foreseeable and caused by A is often an impossible hurdle for the plaintiff to surmount. However this is what our present laws of causation require the plaintiff to do.

Evidence in court

The plaintiff has the burden of proof and in civil cases this must be established on a balance of probabilities. Evidence has to be secured from witnesses, from contemporaneous records, and from experts that a breach of the duty of care, which has caused reasonably foreseeable harm, has occurred. In the past there has been no clear duty for professional staff to notify the patient if an untoward incident has occurred, whether or not it is the result of negligence, and often the patient has been dependent on the altruism of the professional or signs and symptoms which are out of the ordinary. In the earlier cases on disclosure of medical information, the courts spoke strongly against the possibility of patients seeking access to records, in order to initiate 'fishing expeditions'. Access was permitted only if there was already in existence *prima facie* evidence that a claim existed.

This situation has changed, as we shall see when we look at rights of access to records (see *Chapter 4*). In addition, the procedure relating to complaints, and the recognition in codes

12 *Wilsher v. Essex* AHA [1988] 1 ALL ER 891 House of Lords
13 *Loveday v. Renton* (1988). *The Times,* 31 March 1998
14 *Kay v. Ayrshire and Arran Health Board,* 1987

of professional practice of the duty of the professional to ensure that the patient's interests are safeguarded, should ensure that the patient is notified of any untoward occurrence, including the possibility of negligence. Certainly, failure to speak honestly and openly to a patient or the relatives of a patient who has died or of a child could lead to considerable criticism in any subsequent complaints investigation or court hearing.

Difficulties in getting evidence

A recent Court of Appeal case illustrates the difficulty of the plaintiff in getting evidence and proving causation. The plaintiff, Mrs Sellers, was admitted to the Royal Victoria Hospital, Bournemouth with a threatened miscarriage. She was cared for by a consultant, a registrar and a houseman. The consultant diagnosed an inevitable abortion and ordered drug treatment to be stopped and that if there were no miscarriage as a matter of course it should be assisted by drip. The plaintiff subsequently had a miscarriage in unpleasant circumstances. Among other issues, she alleged the drug regime in the drip had been wrong. The trial judge awarded her £2,500 damages holding that the registrar, who was abroad at the time of the trial, was the 'real culprit' for the composition of the drip. When Mrs Sellers wished to call the registrar on his return from abroad as a witness to prove that the original diagnosis of threatened abortion was incorrect, she was refused permission on various grounds, including the fact that she had failed to prove that had it not been for the abortion, the foetus would have survived to ordinary maturity.[15]

There are considerable difficulties faced by a person bringing an action for negligence. Some of these are listed in *Figure 2.2*.

---

15 *Sellers v. Cooke et al*, 1990

Figure 2.2: Hurdles for the plaintiff

---

a. Elements of negligence: duty, breach, causation and harm must be established.

b. These elements must be established on a balance of probabilities.

c. Costs of initiating and continuing a court action.

d. Gambling against a payment into court.

Financing a court action

Even if the plaintiff appears to have a *prima facie* case, with evidence from witnesses, records and experts, the financial risks and costs in commencing action are formidable. Rules controlling those entitled to support from legal aid funds have considerably reduced the number of those eligible. Most potential plaintiffs receive too much income to receive legal aid but too little to finance action themselves with peace of mind.

Recent proposals put forward by the Lord Chancellor recommend the abolition of legal aid in civil cases for personal injury and its replacement by conditional fees agreed with the solicitors. Under the conditional fee system a 'no win, no fee' agreement is made. This means that if the plaintiff loses the case there are no fees to be paid to the solicitor, but if the plaintiff wins the case a proportion of the winnings is paid to the solicitor. Insurance cover has to be taken out to cover the defence costs should the plaintiff not win, and also to cover the costs of expert witnesses and other trial expenses.

Should the plaintiff lose the usual rule is that the costs of both parties are paid by the unsuccessful party. Only a few days in the High Court can result in thousands of pounds of costs. The libel action involving Esther Rantzen of *That's Life* led to £150,000 being paid as compensation to the plastic surgeon who was defamed, but the BBC had to meet costs of over £1 million.

Payment into court

The gambling nature of litigation is highlighted by the dilemmas faced by a plaintiff if the defendant makes a payment into court. If the plaintiff refuses the payment in and the judge eventually awards less than that payment the plaintiff pays the costs of both sides, which can easily exceed the level of compensation awarded by the judge. On the other hand, if the plaintiff refuses the payment in and the judge awards more than the payment the plaintiff receives the larger sum and the defendant pays the costs of both plaintiff and defence. A carefully fixed payment in can put a plaintiff in a very delicate situation, particularly in a case where liability has not been admitted and is still to be established, or where precedents on quantum are few and weak. Where conditional fees have been agreed, there may be more pressure upon the plaintiff to accept any payment into court, even if it is extremely low.

Recent improvements

Figure 2.3 sets out other improvements that have been made that benefit the plaintiff.

Figure 2.3: Improvements to the plaintiff's chances

1. Time limits
2. Multi-party actions
3. Compensation without proof of fault
4. Procedural changes in civil courts

Time limits

One improvement to the chance of the plaintiff succeeding has been the change to the rules relating to time limits. Cases of personal injury and death had to be brought within three years from the time of action accruing, ie. three years from the date of the incident which caused the harm. The injustice of this could be seen in those cases where the plaintiff might not even know within the three years that he was suffering harm in such cases as pneumoconiosis or asbestosis. The law was therefore changed so that time did not run against the plaintiff until he had knowledge that the injury was significant, attributable to negligence, and knew the identity of the defendant. Knowledge includes facts that he/she could reasonably have been expected to acquire.

In addition, the judge has a general discretion in

personal injury cases to extend the time limits where it would be equitable to allow an action to proceed having regard to the degree to which the time limits would prejudice the plaintiff. He must, however, take into account whether the defendant would be prejudiced by waiving the time limits.

Furthermore, it has for long been the rule that where the plaintiff is under an incapacity, such as being a minor or being mentally ill, time does not run until the incapacity is removed. This can mean that cases first come before court many years after the incident allegedly causing the harm took place. Thus, in one case a mother obtained damages for negligence during confinement 17 years after the birth of her twins.[16]

Multi-party actions

An interesting recent development is that of multi-party actions, where many patients who claim to have suffered from the same cause — especially drugs — combine together in one action. Courts have slowly devised rules of accepting such actions and potential plaintiffs may benefit.

Other ways of obtaining compensation

What about other ways of obtaining compensation without going through the merry-go-round of the legal system?

Schemes of statutory compensation

There is an increasing number of statutes that allow compensation without proof of fault. For example, the Vaccine Damages Payment Act 1979 makes available a sum of £30,000 as compensation for individuals who have suffered serious disability following vaccinations without having to prove that any one was at fault. In a sense it is society's payment to those victims who suffer in order that the rest may be effectively protected from various infectious diseases. Even though the payment has increased from £10,000 to £20,000, and now to £30,000, it is woefully inadequate for seriously brain damaged victims in comparison with the financial consequences of such a condition, and indeed in comparison with the present levels

---

16 *Bull and Wakeham v. Devon Health Authority.* Court of Appeal, 2
February 1989 transcript of hearing

of compensation available if fault can be proved and payment ordered through the civil courts. Discussions to increase the statutory amount are currently under way.

Criminal injury compensation

Another form of compensation is through our criminal injury compensation system. Here it would be necessary to prove that a crime had been committed and, for example, a criminal act of attempted murder or gross negligence before compensation were payable. A tariff system determines the amount of compensation for criminal actions payable. This is lower than that paid out in a successful negligence case for personal injuries. The proportion of persons who receive compensation for medical accidents or crimes under these alternative schemes is, however, minute in comparison with the total number of those injured.

Procedural changes in civil cases

The progress of civil cases through the courts is extremely slow and very costly; major recommendations for reform have been made by Lord Woolf in his report *Access to Justice*.[17] He has suggested a streamlining of the procedures for civil litigation, advocating the use of a case management approach by the courts and introducing a fast track procedure for straightforward cases claiming up to £10,000 with strictly limited procedures, fixed timetables and fixed costs. Major changes to the use of expert witnesses are also recommended since conflict between experts is one of the main ways in which the progress of a hearing is prolonged and therefore the costs increased.

Other changes include the fact that cases claiming up to £50,000 must now be heard in the County Court instead of the High Court where the previous limit was £5,000. The sharp distinction between the work of solicitors and barristers, which can add to the costs of a case, is now becoming more blurred as solicitors develop an advocacy role.

---

17 Lord Woolf, Access to Justice Final Report. July 1996, HMSO

Failures in bringing legal action

It is not surprising from a review of the hurdles in the tort system and the lack of alternative, effective systems that a high proportion of potential litigants give up early on or ultimately fail to obtain compensation.

Figures provided by the Department of Health for 1990/91 showed that £45 million was spent by the NHS in meeting claims for medical negligence. In 35 cases damages exceeded £300,000 each, amounting to about £17 million. The remaining £28 million covered about 7,000 cases where the average per case was about £6,500. The same paper reports that about 95% of medical negligence cases are settled out of court.

In July 1998 the Head of the National Audit Office announced that £300 million had been paid out to meet negligence cases, a further billion had been set aside (Ian Murry, *The Times* 21 July 1998).

Removing fault liability

The Pearson report

A Royal Commission (the Pearson) was set up to investigate civil liability and compensation for personal injuries (Royal Commission on Civil Liability and Compensation for Personal Injury 1978). It concluded:

> *We considered the possibility of abolishing tort for two other categories of injury, medical and ante-natal. In relation to medical injuries, it was put to us that it was particularly difficult to prove negligence and still more important, that it was often impossible to ascertain whether or not the injury was indeed a medical injury. It might not be clear whether a given deterioration in the patient's condition would have occurred but for the act or omission complained of. It was also put to us that there were widespread fears that the risk of litigation was proving an obstacle to good and economical medical practice, and that, if litigation became more common, insurance premiums might rise to prohibitive levels. But we did not find these arguments strong enough to justify making medical injuries a special case where*

tort liability would not apply, especially as we received much evidence from medical and other witnesses which favoured the retention of tort.

Very little has changed in our system for compensation since the Pearson report was published. Demands for a radical revision continue to be made. Some have called for the introduction of a no-fault scheme such as operates in New Zealand, Finland and Sweden. Basically, the system provides for those who become victims of medical misfortune to receive compensation without proving someone was at fault. The compensation is funded in a variety of ways usually a mixture of government and insurance based schemes.

One critic of our present tort system, Donald Harris, Director of the Oxford Centre for Socio-Legal Studies, stated at an AVMA annual conference that no improvement in patient care has been achieved by the tort system. He cited research in New York carried out by the Harvard Law School which found that doctors did not alter their procedures in response to specific medical negligence cases. An analysis of the medical records of 31,000 patients discharged from 51 hospitals showed that only one in eight of those who were victims of negligence brought a claim for damages and of these only half succeeded in their claim, the average time between injury and payment being six years.

This may however change as a result of the work of the Clinical Negligence Risk Scheme which is operated on behalf of NHS trusts. Trusts pay into a pool for liability over an agreed amount to be funded from the pool. The Scheme takes into account, when fixing contributions into the pool, the extent to which the trust has implemented principles of risk management within its organisation and ensured that staff have appropriate training.

Alternative dispute resolutions

In the face of the obvious inefficiencies of our present system for obtaining compensation, recommendations have been made for alternatives to the present civil system of dispute resolution to be adopted. These include mediation and also arbitration.

Extending the powers of the Health Service Commissioner

An alternative system, apart from the introduction of a no-fault system, may be to give greater powers to the Health Service Commissioner. His jurisdiction was extended in April 1996 to include matters relating to the exercise of clinical judgement. He is hesitant to investigate the complaint if it appears that the complainant wants to obtain compensation. At present he has no powers to order a health authority or NHS trust to make financial payments to complainants, but he can recommend that such payments are made. His recommendations and reports are submitted to the House of Commons Select Committee which has the power to make further investigations and question health authority officers and members who have shown a deliberate disregard of the recommendations of the Ombudsman. Enabling the Health Service Commissioner, to award complainants compensation may result in more complainants seeking this route rather than taking action in the civil courts. Changes would also have to be made to the present complaints system, since those who are likely to pursue a remedy through the courts are at present prevented from taking a complaint to the independent review panel, the second tier in the complaints procedure.

Need for reform

It is clear that major reforms are essential, not only to facilitate the recovery of compensation by the injured person, but also to assist the health service body faced with meeting potentially crippling claims. Health authorities and trusts have assumed the duty to indemnify injured patients and have thus eased the burden on medical defence bodies in respect of NHS claims against salaried doctors and dentists. Even though structured settlements might reduce the impact of a large claim, some NHS trusts may still find that the burden of meeting claims up to the ceiling agreed with the pool set up by the clinical negligence scheme will severely reduce the funds available for patient care. There is concern too that the pool itself may not be able to meet outstanding claims without major increase in contributions from the trusts. A radical reform is therefore urgently required.

The NHS trusts

How far does the existence of NHS trusts affect the situation?

Clearly the agreement drawn up between provider and purchaser will include standards of quality expected in the delivery of services. Negligence by the professional staff employed by the trust could therefore not only give rise to an action for vicarious liability of the trust because it employed staff who were negligent in the course of employment, but it could also give rise to sanctions being applied by the purchaser because the trust was in breach of the standards set in the agreement. However, this action will not take place in a court of law since section 4 of the National Health Service and Community Care Act 1990 prevents this from occurring. If an agreement between provider and purchaser over the issue cannot be reached the Secretary of State can appoint an adjudicator to determine the issue.

It is also conceivable that if the purchaser has in some way failed in setting standards or making provision, the health service body acting as purchaser could also be the subject of litigation, as well as the provider. While the White Paper[18] recommends the abolition of the internal market, it still envisages a national health service where GPs will be making arrangements with NHS trusts and other providers for the provision of services to their patients. The agreements set up to ensure these services are provided could lay down standards to be met by the providers.

Implications for the nurse, midwife and health visitor

It is clear that the inclusion of the fault element as the basis of the payment of compensation will continue for the immediate future. Crucial to the issue of liability will therefore be the question of what standards were followed and what should have been followed. The practitioner should therefore follow the guidelines set out below:

1. Inform him/herself of the guidelines for any given situation.

---

18 The New NHS: Modern — Dependable Command Paper 3807. HMSO, 1997

2. Monitor the extent to which these are followed.

3. Follow the advice of the UKCC in its Code of Professional Conduct.

4. If conflicts exist between the Code and the instructions issued by senior management, ensure that these are taken up with the appropriate person or authority, preferably in writing.

5. Ensure that training is maintained to develop skills knowledge and competence in the light of rising standards.

Questions and exercises

1. Use the Bolam test to identify the approved practice in any given procedure. What difficulties do you encounter in applying the test?

2. Are you aware of differences in practice and procedure? How would these affect the patient's claim for compensation should harm occur?

3. Try to apply the principle of the Bolam test to the non-clinical areas of patient care. What difficulties arise from this?

4. Consider the advantages and disadvantages which arise from a system of no-fault liability. Which system is best from the patient's point of view? Which system is best from the professional's point of view?

3

The right to give or withhold consent to treatment

Consent to treatment

Trespass to the person

One of the most ancient of our legal actions is that of trespass — any direct interference with land, goods or the person is actionable without the need to prove any damage: the mere touching is sufficient to constitute grounds for legal action. A trespass to the person constitutes a battery if there is actual touching or an assault if there is apprehension of unlawful touching. It constitutes both a civil action and grounds for prosecution in the criminal courts.

Consent as a defence to an action for trespass to the person

The willing consent of a competent person is a complete defence to an action for trespass to the person. (This is not so in the criminal courts, where it has been held that where there is a prosecution for sado-masochistic acts, the consent of the victim is not a valid defence.)

Evidence that treatment has been carried out without the patient's consent will enable a patient to seek compensation, even though the patient has benefited from the treatment, unless specific exceptional circumstances exist.

Still a trespass even if for the benefit of an individual

It would have come as a surprise to the surgeon who, during an abdominal operation, noticed that the patient had an ingrowing toe nail and who altruistically sorted it out to be faced with a claim for compensation to the person. Yet his defence union made a payment without disputing liability. No exceptional circumstances applied and the patient had not consented to this interference to his person.

No particular form of consent required

There is no legal requirement that consent should be given in writing. Consent by word of mouth or even by implication, ie. by non-verbal behaviour can be valid. Clearly, however, if there is a dispute, written evidence is of far greater weight.

Furthermore, if a patient has signed a consent form it is very difficult for the patient in the absence of fraud or compulsion to maintain an action for trespass to the person. In spite of evidence from nursing staff that patients often do not know what they are signing for, the mere fact of the signature on the form would prevent an action for trespass to the person succeeding.

This was the dicta in the case of *Chatterton v. Gerson* (1981).[19] In this case Miss Chatterton suffered chronic and intractable pain following a hernia operation. She was treated by the defendant, a specialist in the treatment of chronic intractable pain. She received two spinal injections. The second caused complete numbness of her leg and considerably impaired her mobility. She claimed that she had not been warned of this risk and therefore had not consented to the operation.

The judge held that once the patient had been informed in broad terms of the intended treatment and had given consent, the patient could not then say that there had been a lack of real consent.

If there is an absence of consent and no exceptional circumstances exist, a trespass to the person action is a powerful remedy in law. Proof of harm does not have to be established; the trespass is sufficient in itself to constitute a wrong.

The patient's autonomy

A recent tragic case saw the death of a mother who had just given birth to twins and had refused a blood transfusion because she was a Jehovah's Witness. It was stated afterwards that there was no certainty that a blood transfusion would have saved her life. However, that chance was not taken. Her autonomy and her belief that there are values more important than life itself were respected and there was no evidence to rebut the presumption that she was capable of making her own decision.

19 *Chatterton v. Gerson* [1981] 1 All ER 885

This principle of autonomy was recently affirmed by the Court of Appeal in the case of Re T 1992.[20] It emphasised that there was a presumption that an adult was competent and therefore able to refuse even life-saving treatment. This presumption could be rebutted if there was evidence of incapacity. In this case a 20 year old daughter whose mother was a Jehovah's Witness refused to have a life-saving blood transfusion and the case was brought to court by the doctors and by the father. The Court of Appeal emphasised that the doctors, in considering whether to accept an adult patient's refusal to consent to treatment which in their clinical judgement was necessary, should consider whether the patient's decision had been intended to apply to the particular circumstances or whether the capacity to decide had been affected by shock, pain, drugs or overbearing outside influence. The court supported the view that the daughter's mind had been unduly influenced by the mother and the court ordered the treatment to proceed.

The unconscious patient with a card

There is no UK equivalent of a recent Canadian case, but the House of Lords stated in the case of Tony Bland, the Hillsborough victim,[21] that were the same facts to occur in this country the decision would be the same. In *Malette v. Shulman*,[22] the patient aged 57 was seriously injured in a road accident and admitted unconscious to hospital. The defendant's doctor diagnosed incipient shock from loss of blood. He ordered intravenous glucose followed by Ringer's Lactate. A Jehovah's Witness card, found in the plaintiff's purse requested that no blood be administered 'under any circumstances'. The doctor, although aware of the card, personally administered blood transfusions he considered necessary to preserve the patient's life. The patient survived and sued the doctor. The trial judge awarded $20,000 (ie. Canadian dollars) to the patient, holding that the card was a valid restriction of the doctor's right to treat the plaintiff which he was not entitled to ignore. The doctor appealed to the Ontario Court of Appeal and lost his appeal — the card

20 Re T (adult: refusal of medical treatment) [1992] 4 All ER 649
21 *Airedale NHS Trust v. Bland* [1993] 1 All ER 821
22 *Malette v. Shulman* [1988] 63 OR (2d) 243 (Ontario High Court)

imposed a valid restriction, even though the patient was unconscious, since the card was intended to cover the situation where advice was not possible. In addition, the State's interest in protecting the lives and health of its citizens and the integrity of the medical profession did not prevent a competent adult from refusing life-preserving medical treatment.

The card read as follows.

Figure 3.1: No blood transfusions

As one of Jehovah's Witnesses with firm religious convictions, I request that no blood or blood products be administered to me under any circumstances. I fully realise the implications of this position, but I have resolutely decided to obey the Bible command: 'Keep abstaining... from blood' (Acts 15: 28, 29).

However, I have no religious objection to use the non blood alternatives, such as Dextran, Haemaccel, PVP, Ringer's Lactate or saline solution.

(Translation from the original French)

In this country it is clear from the ruling in the Court of Appeal discussed above that the doctors would have a clear duty to examine the validity of this written refusal in the light of the particular circumstances of the present situation and, if they had any reason to question whether the statement purported to be the true views of the patient, to give life-saving treatment. They could always have recourse to the view of the Courts (as happened in Re T) but time might prevent this as a realistic possibility. An advance refusal or statement sometimes known as a living will is binding on health professionals if it is clear that the patient was competent when it was made and that there is evidence to show that it would still be valid at the time of the patient's incapacity. The Law Commission[23] suggested that legislation should be enacted to cover for the making, revocation and implications of advance statements of refusal. At the time of writing the Lord Chancellor has issued a consultation paper to cover the whole field of mental incapacity.[24]

---

23 Law Commission Report Number 231 Mental Incapacity. HMSO 1995
24 Lord Chancellor 'Who Decides?' Lord Chancellor's Office 1997

A right to die?

In Re T the court emphasised that what was under discussion was not the right to die but the right of a patient to live as he/she wished and choose the treatment he/she wished; and the court emphasised that this right existed. In certain circumstances therefore the patient is entitled to refuse treatment even if it is life-saving. In the Tony Bland case the House of Lords held that had he, when mentally competent, made an advance refusal of treatment, this would have to be taken into account by doctors when he subsequently lost the capacity to make decisions. In a High Court decision[25] it was held that the court could issue a declaration that prison officers and medical attendants could lawfully abstain from providing food or drink to a prisoner for as long as he retained the capacity to refuse nutrition or hydration.

The right to commit suicide

Since 1961 it has not been a crime to commit suicide. Any person therefore who takes an action to end his/her life and fails cannot then be prosecuted for attempting to commit suicide.

Illegality of aiding and abetting a suicide

However, any person who aids and abets another to attempt or to commit suicide is guilty of an offence. The practitioner can therefore under no circumstances assist a patient to end his/her life. To do so is a crime.

Euthanasia, the facilitation of those who wish to die, is not recognised in the law of this country. The prosecution of the consultant Nigel Cox following his administration of potassium chloride to a dying patient shows the difficulties for the practitioner in this area. Drugs can be given to relieve pain even if they incidentally have the side effect of shortening life, provided that that is not the intention. Drugs cannot be given to shorten life, even if they incidentally relieve pain. The prosecution has the burden of establishing that the defendant intended to cause death or was grossly negligent as to whether death would occur as a result of his actions.

---

25 *Secretary of State for the Home Department v. Robb.* The Times Law Report, October 21 1994

Other defences to an action for trespass

What are the exceptional circumstances that would enable treatment to be given without consent without giving rise to a trespass to the person?

The common law power to act out of necessity

The first is the right to act out of necessity in the best interests of another. This defence was used successfully in a case involving suffragettes who went on a hunger strike while in prison. They were force-fed and on their release sued for trespass to the person, but lost the case. The judge held that:

> *It was the duty both under the rules, and apart from the rules, of the officials to preserve the health and lives of the prisoners who were in the custody of the Crown. If they forcibly fed the plaintiff when it was not necessary, the defendants ought to pay damages.*

The jury after considering for two minutes, returned a verdict for the defendants.[26]

The right to act out of necessity in the best interests of the patient has been conventionally described as the common law power of the professional and has been used to justify a wide range of action where there are no statutory provisions. The House of Lords had the task of defining this power in a case involving the sterilisation of a mentally handicapped woman aged 35 years.[27]

Their conclusion was that in a case where the patient was incapable of giving consent a doctor who acted out of necessity in the best interests of the patient and followed the accepted approved professional practice according to the Bolam test was acting lawfully. Necessity included not just life-saving action but day to day care essential for the patient's well being.

At present there is a vacuum in law — neither relatives, nor guardians, nor proxy decision makers have the legal right to give consent in relation to health care. The carers, both professional and non-professional, can act in the best interests of the mentally incapacitated adult, applying to court when necessary, for example, for a declaration that a sterilisation

---

26 *Leigh v. Gladstone* (1909) 26 TLR 139
27 *F. v. West Berkshire Health Authority and another* [1989] 2 All ER 545

would be in the best interests of the patient and therefore lawful.

The Law Commission, following comprehensive consultation, has recently produced proposals for filling this gap.[28] It has drafted legislation to provide a statutory framework for decision making and also to provide protection for the mentally incapable adult. The present Government has indicated its intention to consider these proposals and a consultation paper has been prepared by the Lord Chancellor with a view to future legislation.[29] In the meantime, carers for mentally incapacitated adults can use the protection of the common law powers recognised by the House of Lords in the Re F case, provided they act in the best interests of the adult and follow the Bolam test.

A recent Court of Appeal decision has ruled that the common law power of necessity cannot be used to admit to hospital for treatment for mental disorder patients who are incapable of giving consent to the admission.[30] The implications of this decision are vast, since a large proportion of the in-patients being treated for mental disorder, such as the elderly mentally infirm, those with learning disabilities and some chronic patients, are not capable of making their own decisions and are at present not usually detained under mental health legislation. The House of Lords allowed the appeal and ruled that a common law power of necessity could be used to admit a mentally incapacitated adult for treatment. It recommended a review of the Mental Health Act 1983.[31]

Two contrasting cases

Broadmoor patient's refusal to have an amputation upheld

In the case of Re C[32] the court issued an injunction preventing any doctor carrying out an amputation of the patient's leg without his consent. Although the patient was a chronic schizophrenic and

---

28 Law Commission Report No 231 Mental Incapacity. HMSO 1995
29 Lord Chancellor 'Who Decides?' Lord Chancellor's Office 1997
30 *L. v Bournewood Community Mental Health NHS Trust* December 1997; Ian Murray 'Mental patients being held in hospital illegally'. *The Times,* 3 December 1997: 1
31 [1998] 1 All ER 634 HL
32 Re C (adult: refusal of medical treatment) [1994] 1 All ER 819

detained under the Mental Health Act in Broadmoor hospital, the court held that he was capable of making a valid refusal to have the amputation, since he had understood the proposed treatment information, believed it and arrived at a clear choice. The presumption in favour of his right to self-determination had not been displaced.

Woman suffering from needle phobia considered to be mentally incompetent

In contrast, in the case of MB[33] a pregnant woman who needed and desired to have a Caesarean section but whose fear of needles caused her to panic in the operating theatre and refuse to have an anaesthetic, was held to be temporarily mentally incompetent and that therefore it was appropriate for the courts to declare that it would be lawful for the doctors to operate on her without her consent. The operation was held to be in her best interests.

The Court of Appeal in the MB case gave guidance on the procedure that should be followed when it was feared that a pregnant woman might be considered mentally incapable of making a decision in relation to her care and treatment.

Powers under the Mental Health Act 1983

Other exceptional circumstances that might justify action which would otherwise be a trespass to the person include Part IV of the Mental Health Act 1983, which enables treatment to be given without the consent of the detained patient in carefully defined circumstances and according to specific conditions. The giving of treatment in these situations is monitored by the Mental Health Act Commission, which has a statutory duty to act on behalf of the Secretary of State in the review of the exercise of powers and discharge of duties under the Act, visiting and interviewing, and hearing complaints from, detained patients.

While the treatment provisions of the Mental Health Act 1983 cover treatment for mental disorder, this has been held to include the compulsory feeding of a patient suffering from anorexia[34] and also, in a much disputed decision, a compulsory Caesarean.[35]

33 Re MB (Caesarean section). The Times Law Report, 18 April 1997
34 *B. v. Croydon District Health Authority* [1995] 1 All ER 683
35 *Tameside and Glossop Acute Services Trusts v. CH* [1996] FL 762

Consent in particular circumstances

Minors

Minors of 16 and 17 years have a statutory right to give consent to treatment including diagnostic procedures and anaesthetics for medical and dental treatment. This consent does not prevent the parents also giving consent for the 16 and 17 year old but, in the event of a clash between parent and child, it would be unreasonable in most circumstances for the professional to act on the parental consent and inflict treatment on an unwilling minor of this age.

   This issue arose in the case of a 16 year old girl who was suffering from anorexia nervosa (Re W 1992)[36]. At the date of the hearing she had refused to eat for nine days, had lost 8 lb in 14 days and weighed 5 st 7 lb although 5 ft 7 in tall. The court decided that it had a duty to override her wishes. The court had power under its *parens patriae* jurisdiction even when the minor was competent (under the Gillick ruling) to make a decision which overruled the minor.

   She had not been detained under the Mental Health Act 1983. Sometimes patients with anorexia nervosa are placed under compulsory sections of the Mental Health Act so that treatment can be given under Part IV provisions. The Court of Appeal relied upon the fact that the girl was only 16 and therefore came under the inherent jurisdiction of the court to care for minors. The fact that she had a statutory right at 16 or 17 to give consent to treatment under the Family Law Reform Act 1969 and for her wishes to be taken into account under the Children Act 1989 did not mean that her wishes could not be overruled if to do so was in her best interests. The Court of Appeal noted that she had not been detained under the Mental Health Act 1983 and appreciated that detention could lead to her being stigmatised. It did not comment that she therefore failed to benefit from the protection that the Act gave to patients treated against their will.

Minors under 16 years

For minors below the age of 16 years parents have the power to consent. However, if they refuse to give consent in circumstances where the child's life is at risk the professional

---

36 Re W (a minor) (Medical Treatment) [1992] 4 All ER 627

would have the right to act in the best interests of the child and in an emergency situation would not have to wait for an order of the court. In addition the Gillick case[37] established that where the minor had sufficient maturity to understand the nature of the proposed treatment and the capacity to make a decision in his/her own right parental consent did not have to be obtained. The court was concerned with the issue over family planning but its statement of principle could apply to other fields of health care.

The Children Act 1989

The underlying philosophy of this Act is that the views of the child should where possible be taken into account. So, for example, section 38(6) states in relation to the making of interim orders:

> *Where the court makes an interim care order, or interim supervision order, it may give such directions (if any) as it considers appropriate with regard to the medical or psychiatric examination or other assessment of the child;* **but if the child is of sufficient understanding to make an informed decision he may refuse to submit to the examination or other assessment** (author's emphasis).

Similar words to those in bold are also included in the Act in relation to child assessment orders (S.43(8)); emergency protection orders (44(7)) and psychiatric and medical examination and treatment (Schedule 3, paragraphs 4 and 5).

In the Re W (1992) case discussed above the Court of Appeal held that its decision to overrule the wishes of the minor suffering from anorexia nervosa were consistent with the duty of the court to make the child's welfare the paramount consideration and was not inconsistent with the sections and schedules cited above.

Research on a minor

There is a doubtful legal situation where consent for research upon a minor is required. There is justification for saying that a parent cannot give a valid consent to research procedures

---

37 *Gillick v. West Norfolk and Wisbech Area Health Authority and the DHSS* [1985] 3 All ER 402

which are not in the best interests of the child or where there is a significant risk. Where the child is likely to benefit from the therapeutic aspects of the research different considerations apply. Where the child will not receive any personal benefit from the research there can be no justification in submitting the child to even minor risk.

Consent has sometimes been given by parents for one child to be a donor for another child, for example in the donation of bone marrow. However, in cases where there is doubt as to whether such donation is in the best interests of the donor child the views of the court could be sought.

Mentally disordered persons

Where an adult lacks the mental capacity to make a decision on a particular issue in relation to his/her care and treatment, on the authority of Re F, the professional should act in the best interests of the patient. Practitioners are sometimes asked to give written consent on behalf of a patient who is incapable of giving consent.

For example, a person with learning disabilities may require dental treatment and the dentist might ask a practitioner to sign the form on behalf of the patient consenting to the treatment. The practitioner does not at present have the right in law to give such consent. Nor does the relative of the patient. If treatment is considered by the dentist to be in the best interest of the patient then he should proceed with it. An appropriate form for such purposes can be found in the NHS Executive's booklet on consent to treatment and is produced in *Figure 3.2.*

Figure 3.2: Form of consent where patient lacks capacity

Medical or dental treatment of a patient who is unable to consent because of mental disorder

Health authority	Patient's surname
Hospital	Other names
Unit number	Date of birth
	Sex (please tick) Male ☐ Female ☐

NOTE

If there is any doubt the ability of a mentally disordered patient to give consent to treatment, the Registered Medical Practitioner in charge of the patient should be asked to interview the patient. If, in his or her opinion, the patient is able to give valid consent to medical, dental or surgical treatment, he or she should be asked to do so and no-one further should be involved.

If the patient is considered unable to give valid consent it is considered good practice to discuss any proposed treatment with the next of kin.

For surgical or dental operations the form should also be signed by the Registered Medical or Dental Practitioner who carries out the treatment.

Doctors/dentists

Describe investigation, operation or treatment involved

Complete this part of the form

In my opinion .... is not capapble of giving consent to treatment. In my opinion the treatment proposed is in his/her best interests and should be given.

The patient's next of kin have/have not been informed. *(delete as necessary)*

Date: ....

Signature   Signature

Name of Registered Medical   Name of Second Registered Medical/
Practitioner in charge of the patient   Dental Practitioner who is providing
                                         treatment

In the case of Re Y[38] the court held that it was in the best interests of a severely mentally and physically handicapped woman to be a donor of bone marrow for her younger sister who suffered from a bone marrow disorder. Account was taken of the fact that their mother's ability to visit the elder daughter would be significantly impaired were the younger daughter to die. It was therefore to the emotional, psychological and social benefit of the older daughter to act as donor to her sister.

Spouses or cohabitees

The law gives no authority to either a spouse or cohabitee to give consent on behalf of the partner even when the patient is unconscious or requiring an operation for sterilisation. It would be good professional practice to get the views of the partner where this is appropriate but the partner does not have any right of veto.

Information-giving and negligence

In *Chatterton v. Gerson*[39] it was held that if the patient had signed the consent form in the absence of fraud or compulsion, an action for trespass to the person could not succeed. Where the patient was alleging that she did not have sufficient information to appreciate the risks involved in undergoing the treatment and she suffered harm the appropriate action was one in negligence not in trespass. The negligence action was based on the principle that the doctor's duty of care to the patient included the duty to inform the patient of the risks and implications of the proposed treatment. If he were in breach of this duty and the patient suffered harm the patient might have a successful claim against the doctor. But how much information is the patient entitled to have? When could negligence be established?

This was the issue before the House of Lords in the Sidaway case.[40] The facts were that Mrs Amy Sidaway suffered from persistent pain in her neck and shoulders and was advised to have an operation. The surgeon warned her of the

---

38 Re Y (Mental Incapacity: Bone Marrow Transplant) [1996] 2 FLR 787
39 *Chatterton v. Gerson* [1981] 1 All ER 885
40 *Sidaway v. Board of Governors of the Bethlem Royal Hospital and the Maudsley Hospital* [1985] 1 All ER 643

possibility of disturbing a nerve root but did not mention the possibility of damage to the spinal cord, which was less than one per cent. She consented to the operation, but the spinal column was damaged and she was left severely disabled.

The speeches in the House of Lords, with the exception of Lord Scarman's, showed a reluctance to take the American road, and the doctrine of 'informed consent' accepted in the United States was denied any place in our jurisdiction. Instead the majority applied the Bolam test to the duty of giving information to a patient.

> *The merit of the Bolam test is that the criterion of the duty of care owed by a doctor to his patient is whether he has acted in accordance with a practice accepted as proper by a body of responsible and skilled medical opinion.*

Lord Diplock, 1985: 657

So, what are the patients' rights to information?

The right consists of being given information about significant risks of substantial harm.

> *To decide what risks the existence of which a patient should be voluntarily warned and the terms in which such warning, if any, should be given, having regard to the effect that that warning may have, is as much an exercise of professional skill and judgement as any other part of the doctor's comprehensive duty of care to the individual patient.*

Lord Diplock, 1985: 659

Therapeutic privilege

Do all patients have to be given this information? The answer is no. The courts recognised the existence of the right of therapeutic privilege.

> *An obligation to give a patient all the information available to the doctor would often be inconsistent with the doctor's contractual obligation to have regard to the patient's best interests. Some information might confuse, other information might alarm a particular patient, the doctor must decide in the light of his training and experience and in the light of his knowledge of the patient what should be said and how it should be said.*

Lord Templeman, 1985: 665

The principles of the Bolam test would be applied to defining the standard of care to be followed in both the giving of and the withholding of information from the patient.

A similar principle has been used in the statutes relating to access to information as we shall see in *Chapter 5*. There is no absolute right for a patient to receive all relevant information. A paternalistic attitude is clearly apparent in judicial and parliamentary thinking on this issue.

Nor is it easy for a plaintiff to succeed in this type of action. The courts insist that the plaintiff establish that, had he known of the significant risks of substantial harm (of which the doctor failed to inform him), he would not have had that operation or treatment. It is very difficult to prove you would have done X (ie. refused treatment), rather than consenting to treatment if you had known of Y, if the possibility of Y had never occurred to you. This has undoubtedly been a major obstacle to claims for compensation succeeding.

The difficulties of succeeding in this kind of action can be seen from the case of *Blyth v Bloomsbury Health Authority* 1987[41] where the plaintiff complained that she had been given insufficient information about the contraceptive drug Depo-Provera which caused unpleasant side effects. The Court of Appeal applied the Sidaway principle and held that:

> the amount of information to be given must depend upon the circumstances and as a general proposition it is governed by what is called the 'Bolam test'. Information that the hospital doctor possesses as a result of her own research did not have to be passed on to the patient.

Clearly, however, if a case succeeds, there is the likelihood of improvements in communication. This happened in the field of sterilisation. In the case of *Thake v. Maurice*, the plaintiffs, a married couple, did not wish to have any more children and the husband underwent a vasectomy in October 1975. In 1977 the wife became pregnant again. They won their case in the High Court[42] against the defendant on the ground that he failed to give his usual warning that there was a slight risk that the husband could become fertile again. Compensation of

41 *Blyth v. Bloomsbury AHA* (1987). *The Times* 11 February 1987 Court of Appeal [1993] 4 Med LR 151
42 *Thake v. Maurice* [1984] 2 All ER 513 High Court

£11,177 was awarded. However, the Court of Appeal in a majority verdict upheld the appeal on the grounds that the contract did not guarantee sterility.[43]

Warnings about the possibility of treatment not being completely successful

It is now standard practice to warn patients that there is a risk that the sterilisation might not succeed and cannot be 100% guaranteed with the usual surgery.

The NHS Management Executive has recently published guidance on consent for examination and treatment; this includes a specimen form for the patient and professional to sign. Separate forms are available for health professionals other than doctors or dentists and there is also a form for a doctor or dentist to sign in the case of a patient unable to consent because of mental disorder (see *Figure 3.2*). This would be based on the principles set out by the House of Lords in Re F and covers mentally disordered patients who do not come under the provisions of Part IV of the Mental Health Act 1983. The form does not cover the situation where the patient refuses to consent because of mental disorder.

Guidelines for the practitioner

1. Has the competence of the patient/client/resident to make a particular decision been determined?

2. What information should reasonably be given to the patient/client/resident to assist him/her in making the decision?

3. If the person lacks the competence to make the decision, who should be involved in advising on the appropriate course of action?

4. Does the professional have the power to act without the consent of the person?

5. If so what is the source of this power?

6. Should the courts be involved?

---

43 *Thake v. Maurice* [1986] 1 All ER 497 CA

Exceptions to the Sidaway principle

While in general there is not an absolute duty to disclose to the patient every piece of relevant information in order to obtain a valid consent, in certain circumstances it could be said that the circumstances justify giving full information to the patient.

Information given to participants in research

It is suggested that where the patient is participating in a research programme then more should be disclosed to the participant of the risks involved, especially where the research has no therapeutic benefit for the participant (Brazier, 1992: 418). While this duty is laid down in the Helsinki Declaration on the code of ethics on research on humans and in the Department of Health circulars it has not yet come before the courts. The argument is that if full information relating to risks and side effects is not given to participants their consent in the research programme has been obtained by deception. If there is no therapeutic benefit to the participant such deceit cannot be justified as being in the best interests of the participant. The Pearson report (Royal Commission on Civil Liability and Compensation for Personal Injury, HMSO, 1978) recommended that those who volunteer to take part in medical research should receive compensation for any harm which occurs on a no fault liability basis. However, this has not been implemented in law, though many researchers may well pay out on this basis on an ex gratia basis.

Information given to those who donate eggs for IVF

It is a requirement that those who donate eggs or embryos to be used in in vitro fertilisation and other techniques should be given full information about the risks involved in what may be essentially a surgical procedure that also requires drugs to induce superovulation. Since the donor obtains no personal benefit, she should therefore have a full understanding of all that is involved before giving consent. Schedule 3 of the Human Fertilisation and Embryology Act 1992 emphasises the importance of free and informed consent being given. The consent must be given in writing and cover the items specified in the schedule. Before the person gives consent she must:

   a.   be given a suitable opportunity to receive counselling about the implications of taking the proposed steps.

   b.   be provided with such relevant information as is proper.

Perhaps these provisions could be useful as an example of the principles to be followed in other information-giving situations.

Questions and exercises

1. Distinguish in your practice the occasions on which you obtain written consent, consent by word of mouth and implied consent. Is there any consistency in the way in which consent is given?

2. Identify the occasions on which you have acted without the consent of the patient. What was the justification?

3. At present there is a gap in the law over the giving of consent on behalf of the mentally incompetent adult. How do you think this gap should be filled? Relatives? Professionals? Lawyers? Others? Give reasons for your answer.

4. The duty to inform the patient of risks is as much a part of the duty of care as that of treating the patient. Look at your practice of informing the patient and consider the extent to which it would comply with the law.

4

The right of access to health records

It comes as a surprise to many that until recently there was no legally recognised right for a patient to see his medical records. Even now there is no absolute right and access can be denied for several reasons.

Data Protection Act 1984

The first legal opportunity came about as a result of the Data Protection Act 1984. The Act was passed partly to prevent damage to our international trade which could have occurred if the United Kingdom were not to ratify the Council of Europe Convention for the protection of individuals with regard to automatic processing of personal data.

The Act covered only automatically processed information relating to individuals; at that time the vast majority of medical reports were held in manual form and not computerised.

An individual is given the right at reasonable intervals and without undue delay or expense:

1. To be informed by any data user whether he holds personal data of which that individual is the subject.

2. To access any such data held by a data user.

3. Where appropriate to have such data corrected or erased.

A recent European directive is aimed at strengthening the protection of individuals with regard to the processing of personal data, the free movement of such data and ensuring common standards across the European Community.[44] The Government has, following a consultation exercise, published its proposals on how the directive should be implemented in

---

44 94/46/EC Directive of the European Parliament and the Council of Europe

this country.[45] At the time of writing legislation is awaited.

Who owns the records?

Patients may consider that, since their medical/health records are about them, they are the first persons who would have right of access. However, this is not so. Historically there has been controversy over who owns the patient's medical records: doctors have claimed that since they write them, possibly with their own pens and ink, from confidences given by the patient, they own them. This is not necessarily the situation. NHS records belong to the Secretary of State and the health authority, acting in accordance with its delegated function, has the right of ownership and therefore of disclosure, subject to law. Health authorities can insist on GP records being returned to them when the patient dies or transfers to another GP, and there is a contractual duty for the GP to keep appropriate records. Breach of this duty could make the GP liable to a hearing for breach of his terms and conditions of service.

Access to Medical Reports Act 1988

The next opportunity for a legally enforceable right of access came with the passing of the Access to Medical Reports Act 1988. This gave the right to an individual to have access to any medical report relating to him which is to be or has been supplied by a medical practitioner for employment or insurance purposes. It came into force on 1 January 1989.

Access to Health Records Act 1990

Finally, on 1 November 1991 patients were given the right of access to their non-computerised health records. The term 'health records' is widely defined: information relating to the physical or mental health of an individual who can be identified from that information and which has been made by or on behalf of a health professional. Information which would be covered by the Data Protection Act is expressly excluded so

---

45 Data Protection The Government's Proposals July 1997 Command
   Paper 3725. Home Office

the two Acts — Access to Health Records Act 1990 and Data Protection Act 1984 — are complementary.

How is 'health professional' defined?

The term 'health professional' is widely defined and includes most registered health professionals such as: doctors, dentists, opticians, pharmacists, nurses, midwives, health visitors, chiropodists, dieticians, occupational therapists, orthoptists, physiotherapists, clinical psychologists, psychotherapists or speech therapists and art or music therapists employed by a health service body. Recently, state registered professions of osteopathy and chiropractic have been added to the list of health professionals. The definition does not however include social workers.

The Act gives a right of access to:
- the patient
- a person authorised in writing to make an application on the patient's behalf
- the person having parental responsibility for a child patient
- a person appointed by the court to manage the affairs of an incompetent patient
- the personal representative of a patient who has died
- any person having a claim arising out of the patient's death.

The rights of access include:
- being allowed to inspect the records
- being given a copy of the record
- receiving an explanation of any terms which are unintelligible without an explanation.

The applicant can ask for records he believes to be inaccurate to be corrected. Inaccurate means, 'incorrect, misleading or incomplete'.

The holder is not bound to comply with the request for correction if he believes the information is accurate, but in this case the holder must make a note on the relevant part of the records of the matters of which the applicant has complained.

Exclusions of right of access

These three enactments might seem to cover every aspect of the patient's right of access and give the patient a significant power. However, all three statutes have similar exclusion clauses which enable the patient to be denied this right.

A health professional can recommend denying access where access would disclose:

i) information likely to cause serious harm to the physical or mental health of the patient or of any other individual

ii) information relating to a third party who could be identified and has not given his consent to disclosure.

There is no statutory definition of 'serious harm to the physical or mental health' and, until there are court cases where a refusal to permit access on these grounds is challenged by the patient, it is uncertain how these terms will be judicially interpreted.

Therapeutic privilege

The Sidaway dicta in the House of Lords permit the existence of 'therapeutic privilege' for professionals to act paternalistically towards patients. There may of course be problems for patients in learning that they are terminally ill or suffering from a chronic condition, but one would hope that health professionals would work towards assisting patients to accept this knowledge, rather than denying them the information. It is thus a question of delaying access to the information rather than preventing it entirely.

Some psychiatrists consider that the therapeutic relationship that exists between the patient and the psychiatrist might be destroyed if the patient were permitted access. However, a request for access might indicate poor communication between professional and patient and feelings of mistrust from the latter. There may well be cases where patients have to be protected against information and paternalism is therefore justifiable, especially in cases of psychiatric disorder; the debate illustrates the gap between those who insist on the patient's right to complete disclosure and those who defend the health professional's duty of care to protect the patient, if necessary, from distressing information.

There are also powers of total exclusion from the right of access under the 1990 Act depending upon the kind of applicant. For example, where the patient and applicant is a child there is no right of access unless the holder of the records is satisfied that the patient is capable of understanding the nature of the application.

Effect of right of access

If patients make use of these statutory qualified rights of access and it is likely that they will be encouraged to do so by patient representative organisations such as the Association for Victims of Medical Accidents, community health councils and patients' association, the existence of these rights may well have a significant effect on patient–professional relationships.

1. Professionals, especially doctors, will be deterred from writing defamatory or abusive opinions in the records, such as 'this neurotic mother', 'I hope I never see this patient again', 'this dollop': these are examples taken from actual records. The advantage is that their negative opinions of such patients will not automatically be passed on to colleagues who subsequently care for the patient, who will thus meet the patient free from the prejudices of their colleagues.

2. Knowing that the patient could have access to his records might encourage some professionals to be more open and disclose information they may previously only have put in writing or told to other professionals. Communication might improve. Professionals may increasingly respect the patient's autonomy and the patient's need to have full information about his condition, including the fact that it was terminal or chronic. In some wards, for example, imaginative use (especially in the care of the mentally disordered) has been made of record keeping to involve the patient in commenting upon his care and making positive suggestions on his future care.

3. Some doctors have said that they will be tempted by the Act to develop a secondary system of records which are kept for their own benefit and are not available to the patient. However, the wide definition of health records would prevent this, since these supplementary, private

records would also be subject to the access provisions. When this is realised, the standard of record keeping of all records may improve. It is not only medical records which are subject to the Act, but also nursing, physiotherapy and dietetic records, X-rays and any personal information relating to physical or mental health which identifies that individual. In other words, all health records made by or on behalf of a health professional.

Nor can a professional hide behind jargon. Section 3 (3) of the Act states that: 'where any information contained in a record or extract which is so allowed to be inspected, or a copy of which is so supplied, is expressed in terms which are not intelligible without explanation, an explanation of those terms shall be provided with the record or extract, or supplied with the copy'.

This sub-section could be interpreted as requiring an explanation if the terms are illegible and thus the professionals could not hide behind bad writing.

4.　The standard of record keeping should also improve because of the right of the patient to apply for correction of the record if any information is inaccurate. An application for correction would initially be made to the holder of the records. However, if the holder failed to comply, an application could be made to the High Court or County Court for the holder to be ordered to comply.

Should there be restrictions on access?

There are grounds for believing that there is no justification for limiting the patient's right of access to his health records, either to protect third parties who have given information and do not want their involvement to be known by the patient, or even to protect the patient. However not all professionals would support this: exclusion does allow for the individual needs and characteristics of the patient to be taken into account. In addition, the appeals mechanism ensures that there is a review of the withholding of records. Many practitioners are finding, even in the psychiatric field, that a more open policy on disclosure of information to the patient does have beneficial therapeutic effects. The nature of the disclosure and how it is handled becomes more important. There are ways of informing patients of bad news sensitively and sympathetically and it would be unfortunate if an absolute right of access were accompanied by callous and cynical disclosure.

A Japanese high court ruled in November 1990 that doctors are **not** obliged to tell patients that they are suffering from cancer. The family had alleged that had the patient and her family known she was suffering from cancer of the gall-bladder rather than gallstones she would not have stopped attending the hospital (since she believed she was not seriously ill) and possibly would have been alive today. In Japan surveys showed that 8 out of 10 doctors lie to cancer patients: they give a diagnosis of stomach ulcer, vaginal cyst or gallstones to avoid telling the truth. However, on the other side of the coin, most Japanese patients, unaware that many cancers can be treated if caught early, prefer not to know. Cancer carries a great stigma in Japan, where it is the country's single biggest killer.

In the United Kingdom there is no settled policy that the patient should not be notified of a terminal illness. Often, in fact, nursing staff find that relatives of the elderly are unwilling for the patient to be told of a terminal prognosis and prefer the professional staff to keep such information from the patient on the grounds that the patient would be incapable of coping with it. Thus, the rule that the patient should be notified of confidential information and then give consent as to who else may be told is not followed (see *Chapter 5*). Exclusion to the right of access should be based on stronger grounds than that the information would be upsetting; the potential for serious harm should be shown.

The right of access to information and records is at the heart of the debate between paternalism and autonomy. At present the law is a compromise: access is permitted, but can be refused if it is in the best interests of the patient himself or to protect a third person. It may be that improvements in communication and emphasis on the patient's autonomy will eventually lead to an absolute right of access.

Questions and exercises

1. Do you consider that the patient should have an absolute right of access to his or her health record?

2. How would you define serious harm for the purposes of the Access to Health Records Act?

3. Are there any conditions where you think the patient should always have access and never be denied it?

4. How has the Act affected your system of record keeping?

5. Can you identify ways in which the right of access could be of positive benefit both to the patient and to the staff?

6. What problems are caused administratively by this right of access? How could they be overcome?

5

The right to confidentiality

The duty to keep information confidential

When we turn to the right of the patient to insist that information concerning him/herself be kept confidential, there are very few cases where the patient has been successful in enforcing it, perhaps because once the sensitive information has been unlawfully passed on there is little point in publicising it further by court action, or perhaps because patients are realistic in knowing there is extreme likelihood that information will not be kept confidential.

Professional codes of conduct

The earliest medical codes recognised the doctor's duty to keep patient information confidential:

> *Whatever I may see or hear in the course of treatment or even outside of the treatment in regard to the life of men, which on no account must spread abroad, I will keep to myself holding such things shameful to be spoken about.*

This is reiterated in the *Code of Professional Conduct for Nurses, Midwives and Health Visitors* produced by the United Kingdom Central Council for Nursing, Midwifery and Health Visiting. An advisory paper which expanded on the confidentiality issue has been replaced by advice contained in *Guidelines for Professional Practice*.

The duty to respect confidential information derives from several sources: it is part of the duty of care which arises at common law and follows from the professional–patient relationship; it arises from the contract of employment between employee and employer, and it may arise from statutory provision.

Exclusions to the duty

The exclusions to the duty to maintain confidentiality are numerous, cause considerable confusion and are endangering the right to confidentiality itself.

Figure 5.1 shows the main exceptions to the duty of confidentiality.

Figure 5.1: Exceptions to the duty of confidentiality

1.　Consent of the patient.
2.　Interests of the patient.
3.　Court order 　　a) Subpoena 　　b) Supreme Court Act 1981
4.　Statutory duty to disclose, eg. 　　♦ Road Traffic Act 　　♦ Prevention of Terrorism Acts 　　♦ Public Health Acts 　　♦ Misuse of Drugs Acts 　　♦ Police and Criminal Evidence Act
5.　Public interest.

No right of privileged information recognised by the court

The court does not recognise any privilege of a doctor or other health professional to refuse to provide information relating to the patient's personal records. An order for production can be made before the issue of a writ in cases of personal injuries or death when the plaintiff or defendant is in possession of that information or after the case has commenced against a third party. During the hearing the judge has the right to subpoena witnesses who can be ordered to bring documents with them. Any rights of confidentiality are dependent upon the sensitivity of the judge or registrar in limiting both the information required to that which is relevant to an issue arising in the case, and the disclosure of that information to within the purposes required by the court.

Statutory duty to inform

Some statutes require the passing on of otherwise confidential information (see *Figure 5.1*). The case of *Hunter v. Mann*[46] is well known for a doctor's attempt to preserve patient confidentiality. The doctor failed to provide details of the patient, who was injured in a road traffic accident, as required under road traffic legislation and was fined £5.

Other legislation dealing with public health requires information relating to infectious diseases to be passed to the community medical officer. AIDS and HIV positive cases are covered by specific legislation.

The powers of the police and procedures to be followed to obtain personal health information or samples of body fluids are now the subject of statutory provision under the Police and Criminal Evidence Act 1984. A recent case emphasised that every factor required by the Act must exist before the disclosure of records will be ordered.[47]

Disclosure with the consent of the patient

The patient can, of course, consent to the passing on of any confidential information and this consent would be a valid defence in an action for breach of confidentiality. Indeed, nurses report the difficulties of maintaining confidentiality when the patient declares his personal details, history, diagnosis and prognosis to the ward or even the world. The recent trend of public figures permitting the press to publish the most intimate details of their health may perhaps result from pressure to maintain good public relations. The announcement of a member of the royal family's admission to hospital is usually followed by details of the reason, followed by frequent bulletins, given hopefully with the consent of the patient. The right to have the information kept confidential gives way to the pressure to tell all. At present there is no Privacy Act which makes the disclosure of private information an offence or actionable. Unless a duty to maintain confidentiality arises by contract of employment, common law duty of care or agreement between the parties, the

46 *Hunter v. Mann* [1974] 1 QB 767
47 *R. v. Central Criminal Court,* ex parte Brown. *The Times,* 7 September 1992

information can be disclosed to the world (see, however, *Chapter 7* and the Human Rights Act).

Release of information as a result of an implied consent by the patient took on an interesting twist in a recent Canadian case. The plaintiff was suing for alleged negligence and tried to prohibit the medical practitioner who was treating him from discussing his case with defence lawyers. The court held that he had impliedly consented to waive his right to confidentiality by bringing an action in which his medical condition was placed in issue. It is uncertain whether the same position would apply in this country and statutory provision exists to compel disclosure to parties within the case, but this does not cover discussions and consultations between the plaintiff's present medical practitioners and defence lawyers.

Disclosure in the public interest

The greatest exception to the duty of confidentiality relates to the passing on of information in the interests of the patient or the public. The former would cover the necessary exchange of information between health professionals caring for the patient, or even to volunteers or other employees if they needed to know that information to protect the health and safety of the patient. However, disclosure in the public interest has rarely been defined and is subject to great debate though it has been recognised by the courts and by the professions.

The public interest — a psychiatric case

In one case[48] a patient suffering from mental disorder obtained an independent medical opinion from a psychiatrist for the purpose of an application to a mental health review tribunal. This independent report advised against the discharge of the patient. The patient refused permission for the report to be sent to the hospital but the doctor did so and recommended that it should be sent to the Home Secretary. The Home Secretary subsequently sent a copy of the report to the tribunal. The patient then brought an action against the doctor, the hospital board, the Home Secretary, the Secretary of State and the tribunal to restrain them from using the document and

---

48 *W. v. Egdell* [1989] 1 All ER 1089. *The Times,* November 20 1989 Court of Appeal

alleging a breach of the duty of confidentiality. The court had to decide whether the disclosure was justified in the public interest and what was meant by that term. In the Court of Appeal it was said that:

> *A consultant psychiatrist who becomes aware, even in the course of a confidential relationship, of information which leads him, in the exercise of what the court considers a sound professional judgement, to fear that such decisions (relating to the discharge of patients) may be made on inadequate information and with a real risk of consequent danger to the public is entitled to take such steps as are reasonable in all the circumstances to communicate the grounds of his concern to the responsible authorities.*

The background to this decision on the nature of the public interest is that the patient had in the past killed five people and badly injured two others. It remains uncertain as to the extent that this ruling can be applied to the non-psychiatric situation. Clearly, a threat of serious harm would have to be established. In cases of extreme danger to the public it could be argued that there is even a duty on the professional to disclose information to the appropriate authorities.

AIDS and HIV

The issue of disclosure in the public interest is seen starkly in relation to patients who are HIV positive or suffer from AIDS. Should the public have the right to know of this condition, eg. should parents of children at a school attended by an HIV or AIDS sufferer know of this condition? Should surgeons and other health professionals have the right to insist on the patient being tested before they undertake their care?

There has been a recent case on the issue.[49] Two general practitioners were diagnosed as suffering from AIDS and receiving treatment but they continued in their general practice work. Information was given to a journalist by a health service employee about their condition as well as the medical records. The health authority applied for an injunction to prevent the disclosure of any further information in the press and disclosure of the name of the employee. The court held that

---

49 *X v. Y* [1988] 2 All ER 648

the public interest in preserving confidentiality of hospital records identifying actual or potential AIDS sufferers outweighed the public interest in the freedom of the press to publish such information, because victims of the disease ought not to be deterred by fear of discovery from attending hospital for treatment; and that free and informed public debate about AIDS could take place without publication of the confidential information acquired by the defendants. The health authority was therefore able to obtain an injunction. However, the court did not agree to an order to disclose the name of the employee because it had not been established that disclosure of the employee's name was necessary to prevent a crime as required by the Contempt of Court Act 1981.

There has recently been considerable public debate over whether there should be a right to insist upon an individual undergoing an HIV/AIDS test — not so much an issue over consent to treatment since at present there is no known successful treatment, but an issue over whether a person can keep his health status unknown even to himself.

The declaration of the rights of people with HIV and AIDS states:

> *People with HIV and AIDS have the right to privacy and in respect of this right, we believe that: information about the HIV status of any person should be kept confidential to that person and their appointed health and social carers (except where anonymous information is given to a public body for the purpose of studying the epidemiology of HIV); information should not be disclosed to a third party about a person's HIV status without that person's consent.*

Uncertainty of the legal position

At present the absence of statutory rights and the lack of clarity on the common law do not give these provisions legal standing.

In spite of attempts by professional organisations and registration bodies to define release of confidential information in the public interest, this is not the law. There is no statutory definition and the few cases which exist are so specific to particular circumstances that it is both difficult and dangerous to define with clarity when confidential information can justifiably be disclosed in the public interest.

Situations such as telling the Vehicle Licensing Authority about someone known to be an uncontrolled epileptic, or notifying the patient's spouse that the patient has a venereal disease, are often fascinating for the philosopher and student of ethics but frustrating for those requiring to know the legal situation.

Occupational health departments

The problems are seen particularly in the field of occupational health. One of the principles of the speciality is the maintenance of confidentiality between employees and the occupational health department; there are codes to protect this principle. However, these codes are not law and there is no certainty as to what information respecting the employee's health is protected from disclosure. Similar problems beset the health services in higher education and probably in other spheres of work, education and leisure activity. The Department of Health/Welsh Office has prepared a Code of Confidentiality[50]. The delay in its production indicates the difficulties in obtaining a consensus view over what are justifiable exceptions to the duty to maintain confidentiality. The Royal College of Nursing has provided guidance for members on confidentiality within occupational health[51] and the exceptions to the duty which it recognises follow closely those recognised by the Faculty of Occupational Medicine.[52] Both organisations recognise that when there is a danger to safety and health disclosure in the public interest as an exception to the duty of confidentiality may be justified.

Confidentiality and European Directives

A recent European Directive is aimed at strengthening the protection of individuals with regard to the processing of

50 HSG (96) 18 LASSL (96) 5 Protection and the Use of Patient Information, Department of Health 1996
51 Royal College of Nursing, Occupational Health Nursing Guidelines, Fact Sheet 11 Confidentiality. November 1996. RCN, London
52 Report of the Faculty of Occupational Medicine: Guidance on ethics for occupational physicians. 4th edn, reprinted February 1997. Faculty of Occupational Medicine, London

personal data and on the free movement of such data.[53] The Government has published its proposals on how this Directive should be implemented in this country.[54] Legislation is awaited. It is hoped that this will clarify rights relating to confidentiality.

Conclusions

As long as the present uncertainties exist, the right of the patient to prevent unauthorised disclosure is severely limited. The protection of the patient's interests and privacy rests upon the attitudes of health professionals, employers, the media and ultimately the general public. The emphasis they place upon the protection of confidential information as opposed to the protection of the public interest will determine the nature of the legislation which will eventually be enacted.

Questions and exercises

1. Consider the extent to which the duty of confidentiality is broken in hospitals. How do you think that the duty could be enforced?

2. Have you ever encountered a conflict between the duty to the patient and the public interest? How was it resolved?

3. Which other health professionals do you think would be justified in having access to the records of the patient in your particular speciality?

4. Identify those occasions on which you consider the public interest will always take preference over the interests of the patient.

---

53 94/46/EC Directive of the European Parliament and the Council of Europe
54 Data Protection, The Government's Proposals, July 1997, Command Paper 3725. Home Office

6

Other rights

Now that the European Convention on Human Rights has been recognised as part of the law of this country, it is important to consider these rights in relation to health care and how they form part of the legal system.

Figure 6.1: Areas covered by the European Convention on Human Rights

- right to life
- prohibition of torture or inhuman or degrading treatment or punishment
- prohibition of slavery and forced labour
- right to liberty and security
- right to a fair trial
- no punishment without law
- right to respect for private and family life
- freedom of thought, conscience and religion
- freedom of expression
- freedom of assembly and association
- right to marry
- prohibition of discrimination
- restrictions on political activity of aliens
- prohibition of abuse of rights
- limitation on use of restrictions on rights

Appendix I to this book summarises the articles within the European Convention on Human Rights included within the Human Rights Act 1998. It will be noted that they include the areas shown in *Figure 6.1*. The first protocol to the Convention recognises, in addition the entitlement to peaceful enjoyment of possessions, a right to education and a right to free elections.

A summary of the Human Rights Act is shown in *Figure 6.2.*

Figure 6.2: Summary of the Human Rights Act 1998

Sections	1 and 2	Definition of the Convention rights
Sections	3–5	Interpretation of legislation; declaration of incompatibility and right of Crown to intervene
Sections	6–9	Public authorities
Sections	10–12	Remedial action
Section	13	Other rights and proceedings
Sections	14–17	Derogations and preservations
Section	18	Appointment of judges to the European Court of Human Rights
Section	19	Statements of compatibility
Sections	20–22	Supplemental
Schedule	1	The Articles: the Convention and First Protocol
Schedule	2	Reservation and derogation

How are the Convention rights implemented within our legal system?

Section 2 of the Human Rights Act provides that a court or tribunal determining a question in connection with a Convention right must take account of relevant judgements, decisions, declarations and opinions made or given by the European Commission and the Court of Human Rights and the Committee of Ministers of the Council of Europe.

Section 3 of the Human Rights Act provides that primary and subordinate legislation, whenever enacted, must as far as possible be read and given effect in a way which is compatible with the Convention rights. It also provides that this does not affect the validity, continuing operation or enforcement of any incompatible primary legislation, or any incompatible subordinate legislation if primary legislation prevents the removal of the incompatibility.

Section 4 enables specified courts to make a 'declaration of incompatibility' where they are satisfied that a provision of primary legislation is incompatible with the Convention rights. This declaration does not affect the validity, continuing operation or enforcement of the provision in respect of which it is given.

Section 5 gives the Crown the right to have notice that a court is considering whether or not to make a declaration of incompatibility, and entitles the Crown to be joined as a party to the proceedings.

Section 6 makes it unlawful for a public authority to act in a way which is incompatible with the Convention rights, unless that would be inconsistent with the effect of primary legislation. It also makes provision as to public bodies which are to be regarded as a 'public authority' for the purposes of the Act.

Section 7 enables proceedings to be brought against a public authority and section 8 enables a court or tribunal to grant relief or remedy if it finds the authority to have acted unlawfully and damages can be awarded against a public authority. Section 9 enables such proceedings to be brought by way of judicial review. Judicial immunity is preserved.

Section 10 makes provision for an amendment to be made by a Minister of the Crown in the case of an incompatibility and other remedial orders.

Section 11 declares that a person may rely on a convention right without prejudice to any other right or freedom conferred on him and also enables any other proceedings to be brought as well as action under sections 7 to 9.

Sections 12 and 13 qualify the right to freedom of expression and freedom of thought, conscience and religion.

The financial effects of the Act

The Act recognises that there could be increased costs for public authorities in amending procedures and also in paying damages to those successfully challenging them. There will also be additional court costs and legal aid but this is not possible to calculate at present. The initial training of judges, magistrates and tribunal members to handle Convention points is calculated to be about £4.5 million.

Other points to note about the draft legislation

The principles will apply only to public authorities and to organisations whose functions are of a public nature, such as charities or voluntary organisations. Those whose rights are recognised in the European Convention but excluded from implementation under the Human Rights Act will still have to take their case to Strasbourg, until such time as the Government in this country incorporates the European Convention in the legal system in its entirety.

The date for the implementation of the Human Rights Act 1998 has not yet been fixed.

Additional non-Convention rights

There are other claims in health care which should be considered.These are shown in *Figure 6.3*.

Figure 6.3: Other claims put forward as rights in health care

1. To obtain a second opinion.
2. To have privacy.
3. To be treated with courteousness.
4. To have one's complaints investigated.

1. To have a second medical opinion

While this right is included in the Patient's Charter it is one which is difficult to enforce unless it can be proved that the doctor (usually general practitioner) was not following the approved standard of care (ie. The Bolam test) in failing to refer the patient to the opinion of a seconddoctor. Similarly, although a patient could request that the consultant he/she is seeing in secondary care should refer him to a similar or different specialist he/she has no right in law to insist upon such a referral. Normally of course the doctor would be happy to make the referral if he was concerned that the patient was not satisfied with the advice or diagnosis and treatment that he/she had been given. However, it is in those difficult areas where there is a refusal to refer that enforcement is unclear. If any reasonable doctor would in that situation have recommended that a second opinion should be sought there would be evidence of negligence, but in other cases means of enforcement other than through the complaints machinery are not available.

Internal market

The situation became more complex when the internal market was established. In effect, the second opinion means two purchases for fund-holding general practitioners, and there may well be a reluctance by GPs, who have the budget to purchase secondary services, to buy another consultation for their patients if they themselves are happy with the initial opinion. The declared intention in the White Paper,[55] that the internal market will be abolished, may not entirely change the situation, since, although GP fundholding may change, the concept of GP consortia acting as commissioning authorities to arrange for the provision by trusts of services for their patients still retains the element of purchase and provision within the NHS.

Second opinion for mentally detained patients

The Mental Health Act 1983 requires a second opinion doctor to be appointed in those situations when a patient detained under specified sections is incapable of giving consent or refuses to give consent to electroconvulsive therapy or where the detained patient has been receiving medication for three months and either refuses to give consent to medication or is incapable of giving consent. Special procedures including a second opinion from a doctor are also required under section 57 of the Mental Health Act 1983 when brain surgery for mental disorder or hormonal implants to reduce male sex drive are being considered. Section 57 applies to all patients, including informal patients. Their informed consent to the procedure must be confirmed by two persons specially appointed by the Mental Health Act Commission.

Outside the NHS

The above discussion on second opinions obviously refers to referrals within the NHS. There is no reason why there cannot be referrals outside the NHS, ie. to doctors in private practice, provided that the patient is prepared to pay for the consultation. It is of course customary to obtain the approval of the doctor currently advising the patient. The advantage of this prior approval is that he/she can make available his records to the new doctor, and any diagnostic tests that he has arranged need not necessarily be repeated since the results can also be made available.

---

55 The New NHS: Modern – Dependable Command Paper 3807. HMSO 1997

2. To have privacy

Anyone who has worked or been a patient on a Florence Nightingale Ward with beds either side of a long narrow room will know how impossible it would be to give patients privacy. As patients have a right to confidentiality (see *Chapter 5*), they could insist that they are not interviewed in a public place where they could be overheard. The curtains around the beds provide little noise-proofing and staff, particularly doctors, on ward rounds are not always sensitive to the patient's need for privacy. NHS patients have no right to single room accommodation. Rules of public decency would normally be respected in providing separate toilet facilities for men and women but there is no right for a patient to insist on being cared for in single sex accommodation. Increasingly the need for maximum occupancy of beds and flexibility of use may mean that men and women are cared for in the same rooms.

There is at the time of writing no Right to Privacy Act. However, article 8 of the European Convention recognises the right to respect for private and family life. It states that:

1.   Everyone has the right to respect for his private and family life, his home and his correspondence.

2.   There shall be no interference by a public authority with the exercise of this right except such as is in accordance with the law and is necessary in a democratic society in the interests of national security, public safety or the economic well-being of the country, for the prevention of disorder or crime, for the protection of health or morals, or for the protection of the rights and freedoms of others.

This will become an automatic part of the law when the Human Rights Act is implemented. However it remains to be seen how generously this right is interpreted and the extent to which it will affect the design and environment of hospital care and the quality of life of the detained patient.

3. To be treated with courtesy

Discourtesy which amounts to a breach of the peace or/and assault where a trespass to the person is feared is actionable in a court of law — either criminal or civil depending on the circumstances. Conduct less than this may well be the subject of a complaint and if substantiated could lead to disciplinary action by an employer against the member of staff concerned.

Professional conduct proceedings could also take place against a practitioner if the conduct amounts to the type of misconduct which they have jurisdiction to deal with. Certainly the Professional Conduct Committee of the UKCC would be concerned to investigate any such allegations against a registered nurse, midwife or health visitor.

4. To have one's complaints investigated

The Hospital Complaints Procedure Act 1985 places a statutory duty upon the Secretary of State to ensure that a complaints procedure is set up in each hospital. The Secretary of State has asked for this procedure also to be available in the community.

A new complaints system was introduced in April 1996 based on the recommendations of the Wilson Report 'Being Heard'[56]. There is now a three stage complaints procedure. The first stage is local resolution, whether by the designated complaints officer in the case of hospital or community health complaints or by the local general practice in respect of complaints against a general practitioner. The second stage is a hearing by an independent lay panel. Assessors from a list held centrally can also be appointed to the lay panel. The third stage is an appeal by a dissatisfied complainant to the Health Service Commissioner who, since 1996, has had the jurisdiction to investigate complaints relating to matters of clinical judgment and also family practitioner services.

Patients who are detained under the provisions of the Mental Health Act 1983 also have the right to complain to the Mental Health Act Commission which can consider all complaints and is not confined to non-clinical matters.

The Health Service Commissioner also has the power to hear complaints about the functioning of the Mental Health Act Commission.

Basic rights of the citizen

In addition, for those patients who are detained under the provisions of the Mental Health Act and who are kept in special hospitals, regional secure units or other accommodation for the

---

56 *Being Heard*. A report of the review committee chaired by Professor Wilson on NHS complaints procedures. Department of Health 1994

mentally disordered other rights should be considered. These are shown in *Figure 6.4*.

Figure 6.4: Rights in secure hospitals

1.	The right to receive telephone calls
2.	The right to have access to a telephone.
3.	The right to receive visitors.
4.	The right to receive mail.
5.	The right to have clothing.
6.	The right to have food.
7.	The right to sleep.
8.	The right to have pain killers and treatment.
9.	The right to have company and not be secluded.
10.	The right to smoke.
11.	The right to have access to books, paper, writing materials and newspapers.
12.	The right to post letters.
13.	The right to see TV.
14.	The right to have exercise.
15.	The right to be treated with dignity and respect.

While the rights listed in *Figure 6.4* (many more could be added: the list is not exhaustive) are not specifically cited in the Articles of the European Convention on Human Rights, many may well be held to be covered by Article 3:

> *No one shall be subjected to torture or to inhuman or degrading treatment or punishment.*

Failure to recognise some of the entitlements listed in *Figure 6.4* might be considered to be inhuman treatment. Others may come under Article 8 (see above).

The duty of care and patients' rights

Of the rights of the citizen which are set out in *Figure 6.4* most would be provided as part of the duty of care. Certainly the right to painkillers and treatment would be covered by the right to a reasonable standard of care discussed in *Chapter 2*. It could also be assumed that the standard of care as judged by the Bolam test would include a reasonable standard of living: food, clothing, society, recreation, exercise and communications with the outside world would all be included in that.

In addition, once the Human Rights Act 1998 has been enacted it may be possible for a patient to show that a public authority has failed to act in a way compatible with the Convention rights, and damages would therefore be payable.

Patients detained under the Mental Health Act 1983

Even though the detention is lawful it does not follow that they can be deprived of such elements that constitute a reasonable standard of care. Most people would agree that patients who have lost their freedom because of a mental disorder should not be punished for this. In a recent case[57] the Court of Appeal held that a convicted prisoner had no right to communicate with the media through a journalist, the loss of that right being part and parcel of a sentence of imprisonment. This principle would not however apply to detained patients. Even if the safety of the public or of the patient him/herself requires the patient to be detained, it does not follow that they should therefore lose all the other rights that a citizen enjoys and which are listed in *Figure 6.4*.

For detained patients there are no minimum standards of care laid down in the Mental Health Act 1983 and related legislation. It is forbidden for postal packets to be withheld unless the patient is in a special hospital and it is necessary to do so in the interests of the safety of the patient or for the protection of other persons. The provisions covering treatment for mental disorder are comprehensive. Provisions relating to the other aspects of care are described in the Code of Practice[58] but this does not have statutory force. Commissioners in their visits can comment adversely when the conditions in which a patient is detained fall below those recommended in the Code. However, they do not have any powers of enforcement. Patients are still found deprived of their pyjamas during the day, patients are still secluded

57 *R.* v. *Secretary of State of the Home Department* ex parte Simms (1997). The Times Law Report, December 9 1997
58 Department of Health *Code of Practice on the Mental Health Act*, 2nd edn. 1995

unnecessarily and very few have an automatic right of access to a telephone. It is possible that the existence of the Human Rights Act will have a major implication for the standards of care for detained patients.

Sexual relations

For the most part the list shown in *Figure 6.4* is not controversial. However, when we move into the area of sexual relationships, there would be no consensus that detained patients are entitled to have sex. Difficulties arise in deciding if this right exists in relation to fellow patients. It is also an issue which causes concern in community homes for the non-detained mentally handicapped, especially where there is a possibility that a female patient/resident is not capable of giving a valid consent and is therefore being exploited. It can cause even more difficulty where patients are detained. Should staff enable detained patients to have sexual relationships on mixed wards? What of homosexual relationships? Would a ward be described as a public place so that any such activity would be regarded as criminal under our existing laws? Or are the bedrooms and bathrooms to be regarded as non-public places so that if the acts take place there by consenting adults then they are not illegal? Yet what is meant by consent in the context of a locked ward where power and pressure groups between patients are common? These are very real problems on which the staff need to have guidance and policies.

Article 8 of the Convention recognises the right of everyone to respect for his private and family life, his home and his correspondence. Does 'private and family life' necessitate a recognition that a detained patient is entitled to enjoy sexual relations while being detained?

Sexual relationships with non-patients

A further problem exists regarding sexual relations with non-patients. If a detained patient is married what rights has the spouse to stay the night in order to continue the marital relationship? The question has been considered for those in prison but has not been explored for those who are detained under mental health laws. At present, many managers of secure accommodation would conclude that to provide such facilities would create an impossible security risk and therefore could not be permitted. Such a blanket policy might not however always be based on fact. The way in which Article 8 is interpreted will have significant impact in this area.

Questions and exercises

1. Are there any other rights which you would regard as essential for the patient's well-being?

2. Do you think that a distinction between the rights of the detained patient and the rights of the non-detained patient is meaningful?

3. Do you think that the law should recognise a right to privacy? What are the implications of such a right for health care?

4. Do you think that patients should have the right to be involved in ward management decisions through patients forums?

7

Patients' rights and the Patient's Charter

Citizen's and Patient's Charters

The Citizen's Charter was published in July 1992. The basic provisions can be seen in *Figure 7.1* and the aims in *Figure 7.2*. This was followed by the Patient's Charter with different editions being published in different parts of the United Kingdom. Common to all are the sections shown in *Figure 7.3*. Since then, local health authorities have been asked to prepare their own charters; an example is shown in *Figure 7.4*.

Shortly after the Labour Government came into office in May 1997 a new initiative on the Patient's Charter was made which would take into account patients' responsibilities. At the time of writing the results of this initiative are awaited.

Figure 7.1: Citizen's Charter

Every citizen is entitled to expect:
Standards
Openness
Information
Choice
Non-discrimination
Accessibility
A complaints procedure/redress

Figure 7.2: Aims of the Citizen's Charter

1. Better quality in every public service.
2. Give people more choice.
3. Ensure that people are notified of the kind of service they can expect to receive.
4. Ensure that people know what to do if things go wrong.

Figure 7.3: Patient's Charter

Patients can expect:

1. to be treated with care, consideration and respect

2. to receive the right kind of service at the right place

3. to be given the opportunity to talk about and to help choose care and treatment

4. to have information in English, Welsh and other languages

5. that relatives and friends will be informed about progress of treatment subject to the patient's wishes and rights in relation to:
   - doctors
   - dentists
   - the hospital service.

Figure 7.4: Example of a local Patient's Charter

You have the right to expect prompt, courteous and considerate service:

- to be addressed as you wish

- to receive adequate notice of your appointment in hospital

- to know the names of those involved in caring for you
- to be advised of any delays/waiting times

- to be advised about any proposed treatment, to be aware of any risks involved or alternative treatment available, before you decide whether you will agree to any treatment

- to be asked whether or not you wish to take part in any medical research or student training, and to know that your decisions will not affect the care you receive

- to receive timely advice of discharge or transfer to enable transport and domestic or continuing care arrangements to be made

- to be treated in clean and comfortable surroundings

- to make your opinions known about the care you have received

- to receive respectful and prompt attention to any complaint you should have occasion to make

- to receive information in English, Welsh or another language

- to have access to your health records under certain circumstances.

Enforceability

How do these provisions affect the law? Are they legally enforceable? At present it appears that the charters do not give any legally enforceable rights in health care, though there is provision in some of the other service industries such as the railways for financial compensation to be made available for failures in provision.

Minimum waiting times

For example, the Patient's Charter sets a minimum time within which a patient should receive surgery. If the patient has waited longer than that, what remedies does he have? From the cases discussed in *Chapter 1* it is unlikely that he/she would have an enforceable action in the courts unless great unreasonableness by the authorities in the allocation of resources and the determination of priorities can be shown. Unless the patient can establish medical negligence he/she could not sue successfully for compensation in the civil courts. The patient does not personally have the right to seek treatment in the private sector and invoice the health authority for that care. He/she might be referred to another hospital outside the catchment area but only if the consent of the local purchasing authority who would have to pay the costs has been given. If he/she belongs to a GP fundholding practice the GP might arrange for him/her to be cared for outside the catchment area by another provider as part of his/her NHS care. These are not however legally enforceable rights.

Value of the charters

Is the Patient's Charter, then, all hype?

In one sense the answer could probably be yes. The Patient's Charter can be seen in the context of the consumerist movement which began with the Griffiths report on the management of the NHS. Griffiths was the managing director of Sainsbury and his recommendations on the general management within the NHS were informed by the view that saw patients as customers or consumers. There is however a huge difference. The NHS patient has no contractual relationship with the supplier of services, unlike his counterpart in the retail sector (and, as we shall see in *Chapter 8*, unlike his counterpart in the private health care sector). The protection given in the sale of goods and services legislation is not available to the NHS customer. There is no equivalent of 'not of the essence', 'not fit for its purpose', 'making time of the essence', which are well established in consumer law. Instead, the NHS patient has to rely upon the Bolam test and the laws of negligence and can sue only when harm has occurred. The charter does not give any additional legal rights.

Lost opportunity

A golden opportunity was lost in the National Health Service and Community Care Act 1990. This Act saw the implementation of the 'internal market concept' through the establishment of NHS trusts who, as providers of services, could establish NHS agreements with health service bodies who acted as purchasers. In the field of general practice, the fundholding group practices take over the role of purchasing secondary services from providers on behalf of their patients as well as being providers to them. These NHS agreements between purchaser and provider do not give rise to contractual liabilities or rights (section 4). There is therefore no way in which these agreements can be enforced. In the event of a dispute the Secretary of State can intervene himself or appoint an arbiter.

The White Paper on the NHS

The White Paper on the NHS, published in December 1997, envisages that the internal market will end and that there will be increased patient involvement through primary care consortia or trusts. However there is no intention to increase the legal rights of patients in the event of services not being available. The patient has no enforceable rights under these NHS agreements. The White Paper recommends certain new mechanisms to benefit the patient. One of these — NHS Direct — is a 24 hour telephone advice line staffed by nurses. This will be piloted in March 1998 with the aim of covering the whole country by 2000. Other institutions recommended in the White Paper include a new National Institute for Clinical Excellence whose membership will include patients' interest representatives as well as health professionals, academics and health economists. A commission for health improvement will also be created to offer an independent guarantee that local systems to monitor, assure and improve clinical quality are in place. It remains to be seen how far these new organisations protect the interests of individual patients.

Standard setting and patients' rights

There is another way of looking at the question. It is possible to see the standard setting initiative of the Patient's Charter as being at the heart of the provision of health care. If commissioners of services insist that providers negotiate agreements which ensure that the terms of the Patient's Charter are included and if commissioners monitor the performance of the providers and look at the extent to which the provisions of the charter have been implemented, the charter may become effective in influencing the standards of health care which exist. The patient would benefit if the standards are met but if this does not happen the patient can only complain.

For example, there is a statutory requirement that after a mentally disordered person has been arrested by a policeman in a public place, under section 136 of the Mental Health Act the patient must be seen by a registered medical officer and a social worker. Some health authorities have set down target times by which the visit by the responsible medical officer to the place of safety must be made and expect the provider of the service to monitor this provision. This kind of term within the service agreement enables targets to be set and monitored to ensure appropriate standards of care are provided. Similarly, the NHS agreements can include reference to the professional codes of conduct and the code of practice issued by the Department of Health in relation to the Mental Health Act provisions. It will then become a term of the agreement that the provider and its staff will be expected to comply with these codes and standards.

Standard setting in relation to all aspects of health care with clearly definable targets has developed within the context of quality assurance and it thus becomes easier to ascertain the extent to which patients' rights are being met. Enforcement will however rest with individual purchasers and not with individual patients whose only recourse at present is the law of negligence, or if there is a breach of the Convention rights action under the Human Rights Act 1998.

The White paper on the NHS published in 1997 envisages that national service frameworks for major care areas and disease groups should be established to ensure that patients get greater consistency in the availability and quality of care across the NHS. The definition of such standards should certainly clarify shortcomings locally, and could support complaints brought by the patient or brought by the commissioners of the service.

On 9 December 1998, Greg Dyke, who had been appointed by the Government to chair an advisory panel to review the Patient's Charter, announced that the panel will be proposing a new charter based on a local approach which will give greater clarity about standards for both staff and patients. He was of the view that the Patient's Charter had failed because it did not give rights to patients, and the majority of people working in the NHS did not believe in it. A consultation document which recommends a more locally based NHS charter is to be published in the spring of 1999. This proposal for local charters however runs contrary to the philosophy of the Government as set out in the White Paper, The New NHS: Modern Dependable (1997) which put forward propsals for national standards for quality across the NHS. It remains to be seen how the Government will respond to the Advisory Panel's consultation paper.

Other charters and declarations of rights

The Citizens' Charter and the Patient's Charter are not the only charters published over recent years in the field of health care. There have been a spate of documents produced by specialist groups; some are shown in *Figure 7.5*. For the most part, these constitute statements as to how these pressure groups would like the law to be changed. They do not necessarily recite the actual law. In the light of earlier sections it should be possible for you to decide which statements actually cover rights that are in existence now and which statements refer to so-called rights that have no legal force. Account must now be taken of the rights included in the Convention of Human Rights and enforceable under the mechanism set up by the Human Rights Act discussed in *Chapter 6* (see *Appendix 1*).

Figure 7.5: Examples of organisations which have produced charters or declarations of customers' rights

Code of Banking Practice — Lloyds Bank
Business Banking Charter — Midlands Bank
Kwik Fit Code of Practice
Water Boards
British Telecom
Electricity Boards
Commitment to Customers — British Gas (now BG Ltd)
Victims' Charter
Education — A charter for parents

Questions and exercises

1. Draw up a charter for the patients in the speciality in which you work. How many of the clauses which you have written cover rights which are already legally enforceable?

2. What do you think will be the impact of the Human Rights Act for hospital patients?

3. Obtain a copy of the Patient's Charter. How many of the clauses are already implemented in relation to the patients for whom you care? What needs to be done to implement the others? How does the charter provided by your local health authority compare with the national charter?

4. Professional responsibility and accountability probably are of greater significance in the protection of the rights of the patient than any other provision. Do you agree and, if so, what support do professionals require to fulfil their responsibilities?

8

Patients' responsibilities

While the emphasis of charters is on the rights of the patient it is important for the nurse also to be aware of the responsibilities of the patient. These are set out in *Figure 8.1*. *Figure 8.2* sets out the sanctions which are available.

Figure 8.1: Patients' responsibilities

1.	To inform staff of medical history, known contraindications and relevant family history.
2.	To carry out instructions on treatment and care responsibly and carefully, or to inform staff if this has not been done.
3.	To keep appointments or give advance notice of inability to attend.
4.	To obey hospital/clinic rules.
5.	To be considerate towards other patients and staff.
6.	To report complaints.

Figure 8.2: Staff sanctions in the event of the responsibilities not being observed (numbers refer to *Figure 8.1*)

1.	Only through the concept of contributory negligence if harm arises.
2.	As above.
3.	As above.
4.	Through the law relating to trespassers and the power to evict.
5.	Probably not enforceable unless conduct amounts to a breach of the peace or a public order offence. If the conduct is offensive, the person could be asked to leave and if he or she fails to do so could be treated as a trespasser and reasonable force used to secure the eviction.
6.	No remedial action or investigation is likely to be taken.

What is their basis in law? The contractual position

There is no contract between the patient and the health professional in the NHS or between the patient and the health authority, whether purchaser or provider. This is because there is no consideration which passes between patient and provider. Even when charges are levied for services these do not form the basis of a contract. Prescription charges, for example, often bear little relationship to the cost of the drugs being prescribed. The drugs are sometimes very much cheaper than the payment being made by the patient and at other times very much more expensive. The patient cannot claim that he/she has contractual entitlements to NHS care. Nor however can the professionals or health authorities claim that the patient has contractual duties towards them. It is not possible therefore to argue that the responsibilities of the patient derive from the law of contract.

Contributory negligence

Responsibilities derive from the civil law and the concept of contributory negligence. If the patient were to bring a claim for compensation and if it were established that the patient had failed to notify the staff of important information, or the patient had failed to follow instructions, it might be held that his/her claim should be reduced by the extent to which he/she has added to the harm that he/she has suffered.

An example

A patient might leave the accident and emergency department with his arm in plaster and be given a leaflet instructing him to return to hospital if there is unusual swelling or pain in the arm or if he has difficulties moving his fingers. These symptoms might occur but be ignored by the patient. If, subsequently, the patient has to have his arm amputated and sues for compensation it could be argued that he must share some, if not all, of the responsibility for what has occurred. Obviously liability will depend on the exact circumstances. Did the staff make it clear to the patient how important those instructions were? Would the amputation have occurred anyway as a result of other causes?

The law of contributory negligence

The concept of contributory negligence derives from the law that a person who is bringing an action for compensation must bear some responsibility for the harm that has occurred if he/she has failed to take reasonable care of him/herself and is therefore partly to blame. If this failure can be proved the amount of compensation can be reduced to reflect the extent of the plaintiff's blame. Sometimes, there could be almost 100% responsibility and therefore the plaintiff would receive no compensation. On other occasions, the blame attributable to the plaintiff would be regarded as so insignificant that it could be disregarded completely. In car accidents, for example, where the innocent person has not been wearing a seat belt and this failure has resulted in greater injuries being suffered than would otherwise have been the case, the compensation payable for such injuries might be reduced by between 15 to 25%.

It follows therefore that the patient has a responsibility to take reasonable care of himself. Staff should be able to rely upon that. Obviously the law takes into account the age and maturity of the patient and any physical or mental disabilities which impede him. Children cannot be expected to be as careful of themselves as adults. Where staff know the patient to be unable to understand instructions further precautions must be taken to ensure that the patient is appropriately cared for.

Nurses' expectations of the patient

What can be reasonably expected from the patient?

The following actions could probably be expected, and failure by the patient to take them if they caused additional harm to the patient could be regarded as contributory negligence:

1. Following the instructions of the professional staff in relation to any treatment recommended.

2. Informing the staff of any contraindications known to the patient before treatment is recommended. In addition, any information relating to the patient's own history or family medical history could be of assistance in deciding on diagnosis or treatment. Being prepared to answer

questions and provide information relevant to the care and treatment.

3. Notifying the staff of any adverse effects of the treatment.

4. Carrying out any other instructions in relation to diet, exercise, smoking and life styles.

5. Keeping appointments and notifying staff if these cannot be kept.

What if the patient fails to follow instructions?

Failure by the patient to follow instructions does not mean that the staff can consider their duty to the patient as at an end. For example, if a patient makes it clear that he/she does not on religious grounds wish to have a blood transfusion, this would not justify any act of negligence by the staff. They would still have a legal duty to take all reasonable care of the patient, subject to that restriction on their activities. If a patient with a severe cardiac condition still insists on smoking this does not mean that the staff can discontinue caring for him even though they might find the patient's attitude and actions repugnant. However, the fact that the patient is still smoking contrary to medical advice might mean that the prognosis following any proposed treatment would not be good and therefore proposed treatment, which would be carried out in a non-smoker, might be considered to be of little value and therefore not be offered.[59]

Are there any other responsibilities of the patient?

The above responsibilities of the patient relate to those actions which would affect the patient's obtaining full compensation were he to bring an action for negligence. However, if there is no action for negligence there is no way in which the law takes account of the patient's conduct and since staff cannot refuse to treat patients who ignore instructions there is no way of insisting that patients act responsibly.

There are other actions which would be considered to be part of the patient's moral conduct but these are unlikely to

---

59 Problems of non-compliance by patients are considered by the author. 'Non-compliance by patients'. *Nursing Ethics* 5(1) January 1998: 59–63

affect any compensation awarded should negligence occur. These include the expectation that patients will be respectful to staff, polite, non-abusive, understanding of difficulties and therefore prepared to wait if other more seriously ill patients need to take priority. In extreme situations some of these could be enforced through laws relating to breach of the peace and public order, and police are sometimes called into an accident and emergency department to deal with abusive patients and relatives. Because of increasing violence to staff, more hospitals are prepared to support prosecution of offenders. In less extreme cases, staff have an expectation that patients will act courteously and politely but this is not enforceable.

Trespassing

In the hospital context difficult patients can be asked to leave the premises, and if they refuse to leave they become trespassers. The occupier is entitled to use all reasonable means to evict a trespasser. Again, this action would only be taken in very extreme circumstances. In the community the reverse is the case and the patient or occupier could ask a community health worker to leave and the health worker would be obliged to go.

Visiting rules

In the hospital context it would be possible to enforce rules relating to which foods and drinks could be brought into hospital through the occupier's right to set down the terms on which anyone is allowed on to the premises. For example, if the bringing into hospital of alcoholic beverages is forbidden, and this rule is ignored by relatives, they could be asked to leave taking their drink with them. If the patient also refuses to obey similar rules, or rules relating to smoking, it could be made clear that he/she can only continue to remain in hospital if he/she obeys the rules laid down by the occupier. This is because in law the patient and the relatives would be classified as visitors and it is open to the occupier to lay down the terms on which the visitor is entitled to come on to the premises. Clearly, account would have to be taken of the patient's mental state, and if the patient is mentally incapable or suffering from mental disorder and this is the reason for aggression or violence treating the patient as a trespasser would not be justifiable.

Dealing with rudeness, discourtesy and aggression

Is there then no limit to the rudeness and the discourtesy which a health worker would have to accept before discontinuing the care of the patient? The duty to provide services is not absolute and if, in providing services in the community, nurses are faced with aggression and abuse the manager would be justified in warning the patient/client and the carer that services cannot continue to be provided if staff are subject to such behaviour. Similar principles would apply where staff face health and safety hazards, such as situations where carers or clients refuse to comply with the findings of manual handling risk assessments thereby putting staff at risk. Clearly services would not be withdrawn until all reasonable action had been taken to secure compliance and to safeguard the health and safety of staff in other ways. Ultimately, however, it may be necessary to withdraw services. Different considerations would apply where the client was suffering from mental disorder and this disorder caused the behaviour. It might be necessary to consider the use of the Mental Health Act 1983 if there was a danger to staff.

Reporting complaints

Another responsibility of the patient is the duty, once a matter for concern or complaint has arisen, to report it to the appropriate person to ensure that it can be properly investigated and any appropriate improvements made. Many patients might prefer to do nothing rather than cause an upset and perhaps cause distress to those staff to whom they are extremely grateful. However, it could be said that there is a duty on the patient to report concerns to management so that it has the opportunity of improving the situation. The duty is not enforceable in law except that the Health Service Commissioner will not investigate a complaint unless it has already been reported to the management so that they have had an opportunity to investigate it. Only if the patient remains dissatisfied can the Health Service Commissioner investigate.

Agreements within a behavioural modification programme and the NHS patient

Even though the NHS patient does not have a contractual relationship with the health service body providing the care, agreements are sometimes drawn up which purport to bind the patient. These are often in the context of treatment for mental illness or in the care of those with a learning disability. They are also used in the treatment of those with addictions. A typical agreement is shown in *Figure 8.3* (see page 91).

What is the legal significance of these agreements? Are they binding upon the patient?

Requirements for a binding contract

For an agreement to be recognised by the courts as having contractual validity and therefore for the terms to be enforceable against both parties the following requirements are essential:

1. There should be a complete agreement by parties having the competence (ie. mental capacity) to make such an agreement.

2. There should be consideration passing from the one party in return for the fulfilment of the promise of performance by the other party.

3. There must be an intention to create legal relationships as a consequence of the agreement.

Can these three elements be said to exist in the context of an agreement in the care and treatment of illness or disability?

a. The agreement

In these circumstances the agreement is usually clear and comprehensive. An offer to take part in a therapeutic programme is made to the patient/client and accepted by him/her. The mental capacity of the patient to make such an agreement is not always verified: if a patient who suffers from intermittent mental disorder makes an agreement while mentally capable to do so is the agreement binding upon him/her when he/she becomes mentally disordered? This point will be discussed below. The capacity of some of those suffering from a mental handicap may not be sufficient for them to bind themselves in this way. On the other hand, there may be some patients who do have the capacity and are able to enter into such an agreement. In the fields of alcohol and drug addiction clear terms may be set down as to the conditions on which patients can be taken on to a particular programme.

b. Consideration

The requirement for consideration means that something must be given in exchange for the performance of the promise. It need not necessarily be money. It could be the performance of a task. A promise to pay another person a sum of money is not binding unless the recipient does something for the performance of the promise. That is why such gifts have to be made by deed which can then be enforced. What does the patient do in exchange for being taken on to the programme? Certainly within the NHS context no money changes hands. Could it be said that the mere fact that the patient undergoes some of the tasks set in the behaviour programme constitutes consideration? Possibly, but as soon as the patient changes his mind and withdraws from the programme nothing can then be binding upon him. In drug/alcohol modification programmes a patient who fails to follow the rules about abstaining from drugs or alcohol could be taken off the programme and would have no right to insist on being reinstated. In this sense the agreement is effective. If the only reason the patient is in hospital is his/her presence on the programme, then he/she could justifiably be discharged or ordered to leave the premises if there were no other condition requiring treatment.

It should be made clear however that consideration cannot consist of doing something that one is already obliged to perform. Patients suffering from learning disabilities who are included in a behavioural modification programme could not be deprived of food, clothing, sleep or other necessities of life since the health service body providing their care would be regarded as having a duty to give those to the patient anyway. The rewards should relate to things over and above those facilities and amenities that should already be provided.

c. Intention to create legal relations

Even if there is a clear agreement between the parties and there is something which could be legally regarded as consideration, the agreement would still not be recognised by the courts as one which would be binding upon the parties unless there was an intention to create a legal relationship.

In commercial contracts the presumption is that there is such an intention, but the parties can specifically deny that fact. In domestic matters the presumption is that there is no such intention but the parties could incorporate such an intention in the agreement. For example, an agreement to pay children pocket money in exchange for their making the beds would not be regarded as having any intention of creating legal relationships and would not be regarded by the courts as enforceable.

It is likely that the agreements drawn up by patients and staff would be regarded by the courts as comparable to domestic agreements and therefore would not be enforced by them. What if such a term stating an intention to create a legal obligation were to be included? The courts would then look very closely at the other requirements to be satisfied that the parties did have the necessary capacity and that there is consideration.

Agreements overriding patients' consent

What is the significance in law of those agreements that have been drawn up by doctors in which patients at a time when they are mentally well agree to undergo treatment and give consent to treatment being given when they are mentally disordered, and at the time of administration refuse to take it. They also agree in this document to give a certain period of notice — perhaps 48 hours — before cancelling the agreement. If, in reliance on the patient's signature to such a document, treatment is given forcibly against the patient's wishes would the document protect the professional staff against an action for trespass to the person? An example is given in *Figure 8.3*.

Such a question does not seem to have come before the courts. The Power of Attorney Act 1971, under which a person could appoint an agent to act in relation to his/her affairs, stated that the agency ended if the appointer became mentally disordered. Since this is often the very time that an agent is required the Enduring Powers of Attorney Act 1985 was passed which enabled the agency to continue and not end if mental disorder occurred. However, very strict procedures have to be followed for an enduring power to be created. It is not thought that this Act could apply to treatment and health care, and therefore a binding consent to treatment could not be covered by these statutory provisions.

Figure 8.3: An attempt at limiting the patient's freedom to refuse treatment at a later date

> I,... being mentally competent know that there are occasions when I become mentally disordered and at such times I refuse treatment which is in my best interests. I therefore request my responsible medical officer Dr... to ignore my refusal to take recommended treatment when I am mentally disordered and continue to administer such treatment against my will. I hereby agree to give at least 48 hours notice of my intentions to terminate this consent.

Even in the absence of statutory provision could the contract be seen as valid at common law?

The answer in relation to patients detained under the provisions of the Mental Health Act 1983 is probably '**no**'. Such a contract would drive a horse and cart through the detailed provisions for protecting patients against compulsory treatment when they either refuse consent or are incapable of consenting. Second opinion appointed doctors must examine the patient and agree with the proposed treatment. Requirements in relation to the documentation which must be kept are stringent and must be monitored.

It is doubtful if such a contract would be seen as binding upon the informal patient. Detention provides considerable statutory protection for those compelled to have treatment and the informal patient would not have this protection. However the point has still to be tested in court. In the meantime, professionals would be wise not to rely on such documents.

Failure to keep appointments without prior notification

As pressures for improved efficiency increase, the failure of the patient to attend an out-patient clinic without prior notification of that possibility can cause a waste of staff time and therefore an inefficient use of resources. As fees have been levied for health services, eg. dental, some practitioners have charged patients for their failure to attend. Where fees are not payable this sanction is not of course available but there are suggestions that some sanctions should be available if it is thought that patients misuse the services in some way.

In the private sector fees for failure to attend are well established and might be payable even when the client has given advance notice.

See *Figure 8.4* for action which staff can take to encourage patients to be more responsible, and *Figure 8.5* for limits to their action.

Figure 8.4: Action staff can take to obtain greater responsibility from patients

1. Leaflets/written instructions/written advice against premature discharge and other treatment and care.
2. Warnings about contributory negligence.
3. Rules relating to visiting and in-patients' or relatives' information handbooks.

Figure 8.5: Action staff cannot take to impose responsibility upon patients

1. Staff cannot withdraw care.
2. Staff cannot impose fines.
3. Staff cannot lower standards of care to which the patient is entitled.

The private patient

All that has been said above applies to the private patient who is receiving care outside the NHS. However, in addition there is a contractual relationship between the private patient and those providing services. Sometimes the patient may be paying personally; more often the fees are paid through insurance cover and the insurance company may or may not manage the premises on which the care is given. This contractual relationship is absent in the relationship between the NHS patient and the health service body providing treatment and care.

There would be in the relationship between private patient and the provider of care those three elements discussed above which are essential for an agreement to be valid in law. The contract permits the inclusion of terms which cover not only the responsibilities to the patient but also any responsibilities owed by the patient. The contract could therefore cover all the responsibilities of the patient in relation to the disclosure of relevant information, and in following instructions, and also the conduct expected of the patient. Such contractual terms would be binding on the patient. If, however, the patient were to be injured or suffer as a result of an act of negligence, the liability of the staff would not be excluded as a result of the patient's failures because of the effect of the Unfair Contract Terms Act 1977. The failures would be taken into account in assessing any contributory negligence as discussed above.

Conclusions

Staff have been rightly concerned in the past that the main emphasis of the patients' rights movement and the patients' charters is to identify rights which the patients have and that there has been little concern with any responsibilities which the patient has. The reciprocal nature of the health care relationship has recently been highlighted in the new initiative launched by the Labour Government in 1997 to lead to the formulation of a new Patient's Charter (to be published in spring 1999) which emphasises the responsibilities of the patient.

Questions and exercises

1. At present there is a distinction between the legal position of the NHS patient and the private patient? Can you think of any ways in which the NHS patient can be given as much protection as the private patient? Are there any advantages (apart from financial) which the NHS patient has compared to the private patient?

2. How can the nurse make it clear that the patient has personal responsibilities for his health and well-being?

3. In extreme situations the patient could be asked to leave the ward. Identify from your own experience the events which could give rise to such a request being made. What procedures and guidelines do you think should be set down to ensure that the patient's rights are protected? If you work in the community, identify the circumstance in which you could be asked to leave a patient's house and consider the action you would then take.

4. The list of responsibilities identified here does not necessarily cover every one. Are there any others which you consider important?

Conclusion

Perhaps patients' rights and the law are wrongly juxtaposed. After all, what can the law do? It can usually only provide a remedy after the event, when death or personal injury has already occurred. Financial compensation is a poor remedy for the loss of life, limb and dignity and for pain and suffering.

The real protection of rights is perhaps not the law, but is twofold: firstly, the individual patient's belief in his/her status and position; and secondly, the recognition by health care professionals that patients should be treated with respect, consideration and humanity and have their autonomy recognised. Both these factors are essential. Frequently patients becomes institutionalised and are prepared to give up autonomy ('whatever you think doctor'); instances of the wrong patients being wheeled down to surgery because of reluctance to challenge staff are not uncommon. Staff have difficulties in respecting and deferring to those who have so little self-esteem.

On the other hand, professional standards of care, professional accountability and responsibility and professional acknowledgement of patients' rights are one of the most important forms of protection for the patient. We should all recognise the sentiment expressed by Susan Sontag:

> *Illness is the night-side of life, a more onerous citizenship. Everyone who is born holds dual citizenship, in the kingdom of the well and in the kingdom of the sick. Although we all prefer to use only the good passport, sooner or later each of us is obliged at least for a spell, to identify ourselves as citizens of that other place.*[60]

It behoves us all, therefore, to recognise and protect the rights and responsibilities of patients, for in so doing we are protecting ourselves.

---

60 (1984) quoted in *Woman Talk*. Compiled by: Brown M, O'Connor A. Futura, London

References

1. The New NHS: Modern Dependable Command Paper 3807. IIMSO 1997

2. R. Cambridge District Health Authority, ex parte B Court of Appeal. *The Times Law Report*, March 15 1995

3. Michael Horsnell 'Refusal to give MS victim new drug was illegal'. *The Times*, 12 July 1997

4. Re T (a minor) (wardship: medical treatment) [1997] 1 All ER 906

5. Peter Singh 'Community Care: Britain's other lottery'. Mencap 1995

6. *Bolam v. Friern Hospital Management Committee* [1957] 2 All ER 118

7. *Whitehouse v. Jordan* [1981] 1 All ER 635

8. *Maynard v. W Midlands Regional Health Authority* HL [1985] 1 All ER 635

9. *Bolitho v. City and Hackney Health Authority. The Times Law Report*, 27 November 1997

10. United Kingdom Central Council for Nursing, Midwifery and Health Visiting, *Scope of Professional Practice* 1992

11. Court of Appeal in the case of *Wilsher v. Essex* AHA [1986] 3 All ER 801

12. *Wilsher v. Essex* AHA [1988] 1 All ER 891 House of Lords

13. *Loveday v. Renton* (1988). *The Times*, 31 March 1998

14. *Kay v. Ayrshire and Arran Health Board,* 1987

15. *Sellers v. Cooke et al* 1990

16. *Bull and Wakeham v. Devon Health Authority.* Court of Appeal, 2 February 1989 transcript of hearing

17. Lord Woolf, Access to Justice Final Report. July 1996, HMSO

18. The New NHS: Modern — Dependable Command Paper 3807. HMSO 1997

19. *Chatterton v. Gerson* [1981] 1 All ER 885

20. Re T (adult: refusal of medical treatment) [1992] 4 All ER 649

21. *Airedale NHS Trust v. Bland* [1993] 1 All ER 821

22. *Malette v. Shulman* [1988]63 OR (2d) 243 (Ontario High Court)

23. Law Commission Report Number 231 Mental Incapacity. HMSO 1995

24. Lord Chancellor 'Who Decides?' Lord Chancellor's Office 1997

25. *Secretary to State for the Home Department v. Robb.* The Times Law Report, October 21 1994

26. *Leigh v. Gladstone* (1909) 26 TLR 139

27. *F. v. West Berkshire Health Authority and another* [1989] 2 All ER 545

28. Law Commission Report No 231 Mental Incapacity. HMSO 1995

29. Lord Chancellor 'Who Decides?' Lord Chancellor's Office 1997

30. *L. v. Bournewood Community mental Health NHS Trust* December 1997; Ian Murray Mental patients being held in hospital illegally. *The Times,* 3 December 1997: 1

31. Mental Health Act 1983 [1998] 1 All ER 634HL

32. Re C (adult: refusal of medical treatment) [1994] 1 All ER 819

33. In re MB (Caesarean section). *The Times Law Report* 18 April 1997

34. *B. v. Croydon District Health Authority* [1995] 1 All ER 683

35. *Tameside and Glossop Acute Services Trusts v. CH* (a patient) [1996] 1 FLR 762

36. Re W (a minor) (medical treatment) [1992] 4 All ER 627

37. *Gillick v. West Norfolk and Wisbech Area Health Authority and the DHSS* [1985] 3 All ER 402

38. Re Y (Mental Incapacity: Bone Marrow Transplant) [1996] 2 FLR 787

39. *Chatterton v. Gerson* [1981] 1 All ER 885

40. *Sidaway v. Board of Governors of the Bethlem Royal Hospital and the Maudsley Hospital* [1985] 1 All ER 643

41. *Blyth v. Bloomsbury AHA* (1987). *The Times,* 11 February 1987 Court of Appeal [1993] 4 Med LR 151

42. *Thake v. Maurice* [1984] 2 All ER 513 High Court

43. *Thake v. Maurice* [1986] 1 All ER 497 CA

44. 94/46/EC Directive of the European Parliament and the Council of Europe

45. Data Protection, The Government's Proposals, July 1997. Command Paper 3725. Home Office

46. *Hunter v. Mann* [1974] 1 QB 767

47. *R. v. Central Criminal Court,* ex parte Brown. *The Times,* 7 September 1992

48. *W.v. Egdell* [1989] 1 All ER 1089. *The Times,* November 20 1989 Court of Appeal

49. *X. v. Y* [1988] 2 All ER 648

50. HSG (96) 18 LASSL (96) 5 Protection and the Use of Patient Information, Department of Health, 1996

51. Royal College of Nursing, Occupational Health Nursing Guidelines, Fact Sheet 11 Confidentiality. November 1996. RCN, London

52. Report of the Faculty of Occupational Medicine: Guidance on ethics for occupational physicians. 4th edn, reprinted February 1997. Faculty of Occupational Medicine, London

53. 94/46/EC Directive of the European Parliament and the Council of Europe

54. Data Protection, The Government's Proposals, July 1997, Command Paper 3725. Home Office

55. The New NHS: Modern — Dependable Command Paper 3807. HMSO 1997

56. *Being Heard*. A report of the review committee chaired by Professor Wilson on NHS complaints' procedures. Department of Health 1994

57. *R. v. Secretary of State of the Home Department* ex parte Simms (1997). *The Times Law Report*, December 9 1997

58. Department of Health *Code of Practice on the Mental Health Act*, 2nd edn 1995

59. Problems of non-compliance by patients are considered by the author. B Dimond. 'Non-compliance by patients'. *Nursing Ethics* **5** (1) January 1998 : 59–63

60. (1984) quoted in *Woman Talk*. Compiled by Brown M, O'Connor A. Futura, London

Further reading

Beauchamp TL, Childress JE (1989) *Principles of Biomedical Ethics*. Oxford University Press, Oxford

Beddard R (1992) *Human Rights and Europe*. 3rd edn. Grotius, Cambridge

Brazier M (1992) *Medicines, Patients and the Law*. 2nd edn. Penguin, London

Cartwright A (1967) *Patients and their Doctors*. Routledge and Kegan Paul, London

Cohen DR, Henderson J (1988) *Health Prevention and Economics*. Oxford University Press, Oxford

Dimond BC (1995) *Legal Aspects of Nursing*. 2nd edn. Prentice Hall, Hemel Hempstead

Dimond BC (1997) *Legal Aspects of Care in the Community*. Macmillan, London

Dimond BC (1996) *Legal Aspects of Child Health Care*. Mosby, London

Hepple BA, Matthews MH (1991) *Tort Cases and Materials*. Butterworth, London

Illich I (1975) *Medical Nemesis*. Pantheon Books, New York

Jansen AR (1990) *The New Medicine and the Old Ethics*. Harvard University Press, Boston

Law Commission Report (1995) *No 231 Mental Incapacity*. HMSO, London

Mason J, McCall S (1990) *Law and Medical Ethics*. Butterworth, London

Morgan D, Lee RG (1991) *Human Fertilisation and Embryology Act 1990*. Blackstone, London

Murphy E (1991) *After the Asylums*. Faber and Faber, London

Rowson R (1990) *An Introduction to Ethics for Nurses*. Scutari Press, London

Townsend P (ed) (1982) *Inequalities in Health; The Black Report*. Penguin, London

Tschudin V (1981) *Ethics in Nursing*. Heinemann, London

Tschudin V, Marks MD (1993) *Ethics: a Primer for Nurses*. Baillière Tindall, London

UKCC publications:

 Code of Professional Conduct 1992
 Scope of Professional Practice 1992
 Guidelines for Professional Practice 1996

Young AP (1994) *Law and Professional Conduct in Nursing.* 2nd edn. Scutari Press, London

White R, Carr P, Lowe N (1991) *A Guide to the Children Act 1989.* Butterworth, London

Reference could also be made to the service provided by Meditec from whom a bibliography of nursing books is available: Meditec, York House, 26 Bourne Road, Colsterworth, Lincs, NG33 5JE; tel 01476 860281

Glossary

Act	(of parliament), Statute.
Actionable per se	A court action where the plaintiff does not have to show loss, damage or harm to obtain compensation, eg. an action for trespass to the person.
AVMA	Association for Victims of Medical Accidents.
Balance of probabilities	The standard of proof in civil proceedings.
Black Report	The report of the committee chaired by Sir Donald Black on inequalities in health which reported in 1980. Reprinted in Townsend P, Davidson N (1982) *Inequalities in Health*, Penguin Books, London.
Bolam test	The test laid down by Judge McNair in the case of *Bolam* v. *Friern* HMC on the standard of care expected of a professional in cases of alleged negligence.
Burden of proof	The duty of a party to litigation to establish the facts; or the duty on the prosecution to prove the facts of the offence.
Common law	Law which derives from decisions of judges in individual cases. Also known as case law or judge made law. Contrast with law laid down by statute (see statutory).
CHC	Community Health Council.

Deed	A written document indicating that it is intending to act as a deed. (It no longer needs to be under seal.) A deed of gift is effective without consideration.
Detained patients	Those detained under the provisions of the mental health legislation. (In England and Wales, Mental Health Act 1983.)
Dictum	An observation by a judge on a point of law arising in the case before him or her.
ECT	Electroconvulsive therapy.
Re F ruling	A professional who acts in the best interests of an incompetent person who is incapable of giving consent does not act unlawfully if he follows the accepted standard of care according to the Bolam Test.
Health authority	A statutory body appointed by the Secretary of State to purchase health services for persons within its district. It is also responsible for managing contracts with general practitioners, dentists and pharmacists for the provision of NHS services within its district.
Health Service Commissioner	A person appointed to investigate complaints arising in the NHS. Sometimes known as the Ombudsman.
Iatrogenic	Illness/medical condition caused by earlier medical treatment.
Internal market	A concept implemented following the NHS and Community Care Act 1990 that there should be purchasers and providers of health care within each district. The White Paper on the NHS published in 1997 for England envisages the internal market ending.

Legislation	Acts of Parliament (statutes) and statutory instruments which define the law.
Limitation of time	A defence which can be raised when the time limits set for bringing an action have been exceeded (see text for many exceptions to the time limits).
Parens patriae	The right of the court to act on behalf of children.
Payment into court	A payment by a defendant into an account maintained by the court in satisfaction of the claim. The plaintiff can accept and the defendant will then be liable to the costs. If the plaintiff refuses and the judge awards the same or less than the sum paid in, the plaintiff is liable to pay the defendant's costs from the date of the payment in. The judge must be notified of the payment in.
Plaintiff	One who brings an action in the civil courts usually for compensation.
Pleadings	The documents which pass between the parties to a court action which set out the claim and the defences and other particulars before the court hearing takes place. The aim is to identify the issues between the parties to reduce or eventually eliminate the need for hearing.
Practitioner	Term used to describe nurses, midwives and health visitors.
Precedent	Ruling established by a court that may be binding upon courts hearing similar disputes at a later time. (A hierarchy of courts determines which rulings are binding on subsequent court hearings.)

Prima facie	At first sight. Phrase used to denote that there would appear to be sufficient evidence brought by one party to require the other party to provide a defence.
Provider	A health service body which agrees to provide specific health services
Purchaser	A health service body which contracts with a provider for specific health services to be provided.
QALY	Quality adjusted life years. A formula used by health economists to contrast the value of different forms of treatment.
Quantum	The amount of compensation, or the monetary value of a claim.
Subpoena	An order to a person to appear in court on a certain day to give evidence. A subpoena ad testificandum requires the person to give evidence; a subpoena duces tecum requires the person to produce particular documents that are required as evidence.
Statutory	Laid down by Act of Parliament (term often used to contrast with common law).
Tort	A civil wrong excluding breach of contract. It includes: negligence, trespass (to the person, goods or land), nuisance, breach of statutory duty and defamation.
Trespass	An action which can be brought in the civil courts alleging direct interference with land, goods or the person of the plaintiff. Harm does not have to be proved, ie. it is actionable per se.
UKCC	United Kingdom Central Council for Nursing, Midwifery and Health Visiting.

Appendix I — Schedule to the Human Rights Act 1998

The Convention Rights (relevant articles of the European Convention on Human Rights)

Article 2
Right to life

1. Everyone's right to life shall be protected by law. No one shall be deprived of his life intentionally save in the execution of a sentence of a court following his conviction of a crime for which this penalty is provided by law.

2. Deprivation of life shall not be regarded as inflicted in contravention of this article when it results from the use of force which is no more than absolutely necessary:
   a) in defence of any person from unlawful violence
   b) in order to effect a lawful arrest or to prevent the escape of a person lawfully detained
   c) in action lawfully taken for the purpose of quelling a riot or insurrection.

Article 3
Prohibition of torture

No one shall be subjected to torture or to inhuman or degrading treatment or punishment.

Article 4
Prohibition of salvery and forced labour

1. No one shall be held in slavery or servitude.

2. No one shall be required to perform forced or compulsory labour.

3. For the purpose of this article the term 'forced or compulsory labour' shall not include:
   a) any work required to be done in the ordinary course of detention imposed according to the provisions of Article 5 of this Convention or during conditional release from such detention
   b) any service of a military character or, in case of conscientious objectors in countries where they are recognised, service exacted instead of compulsory military service

c) any work of service which forms part of normal civic obligations.

Article 5
Right to liberty and security

1. Everyone has the right to liberty and security of person. No one shall be deprived of his liberty save in the following cases and in accordance with a procedure prescribed by law:

a) the lawful detention of a person after conviction by a competent court

b) the lawful arrest or detention of a person for non-compliance with the lawful order of a court or in order to secure the fulfilment of any obligation prescribed by law

c) the lawful arrest or detention of a person effected for the purpose of bringing him before the competent legal authority on reasonable suspicion of having committed an offence or when it is reasonably considered necesary to prevent his committing an offence or fleeing after having done so

d) the detention of a minor by lawful order for the purpose of educational supervision or his lawful detention for the purpose of bringing him before the competent legal authority

e) the lawful detention of persons for the prevention of the spreading of infectious diseases, of persons of unsound mind, alcoholics or drug addicts or vagrants

f) the lawful arrest or detention of a person to prevent his effecting an unauthorised entry into the country or of a person against whom action is being taken with a view to deportation or extradition.

2. Everyone who is arrested shall be informed promptly, in a language which he understands, of the reasons for his arrest and of any charge against him.

3. Everyone arrested or detained in accordance with the provisions of paragraph 1c) of this article shall be brought promptly before a judge or other officer authorised by law to exercise judicial power and shall be entitled to trial within a reasonable time or to release pending trial. Release may be conditioned by guarantees to appear for trial.

4. Everyone who is deprived of his liberty by arrest or detention shall be entitled to take proceedings by which the lawfulness of his detention shall be decided speedily by a court and his release ordered if the detention is not lawful.

5. Everyone who has been the victim of arrest or detention in contravention of the provisions of this article shall have an enforceable right to compensation.

Article 6
Right to a fair trial

1. In the determination of his civil rights and obligations or of any criminal charge against him, everyone is entitled to a fair and public hearing within a reasonable time by an independent and impartial tribunal established by law. Judgment shall be pronounced publicly but the press and public may be excluded from all or part of the trial in the interests of morals, public order or national security in a democratic society, where the interests of juveniles or the protection of the private life of the parties so require, or to the extent strictly necessary in the opinion of the court in special circumstances where publicity would prejudice the interests of justice.

2. Everyone charged with a criminal offence shall be presumed innocent until proved guilty according to law.

3. Everyone charged with a criminal offfence has the following minimum rights:
   a) to be informed promptly, in a language which he understands and in detail, of the nature and cause of the accusation against him
   b) to have adequate time and facilities for the preparation of his defence
   c) to defend himself in person or through legal assistance of his own choosing or, if he has not sufficient means to pay for legal asistance, to be given it free when the interests of justice so require
   d) to examine or have examined witnesses against him and to obtain the attendance and examination of witnesses on his behalf under the same conditions as witnesses against him
   e) to have the free assistance of an interpreter if he cannot understand or speak the language used in court.

Article 7
No punishment without law

1. No one shall be held guilty of any criminal offence on account of any act or omission which did not constitute a criminal offence under national or international law at the time when it was committed. Nor shall a heavier penalty be imposed than the one that was applicable at the time the criminal offence was committed.

2. This article shall not prejudice the trial and punishment of any person for any act or omission which, at the time when it was committed, was criminal according to the general principles of law recognised by civilised nations.

Article 8
Right to respect for private and family life

1. Everyone has the right to respect for his private and family life, his home and his correspondence.

2. There shall be no interference by a public authority with the exercise of this right except such as is in accordance with the law and is necessary in a democratic society in the interests of national security, public safety or the economic well-being of the country, for the prevention of disorder or crime, for the protection of health or morals, or for the protection of the rights and freedoms of others.

Article 9
Freedom of thought, conscience and religion

1. Everyone has the right to freedom of thought, conscience and religion; this right includes freedom to change his religion or belief and freedom, either alone or in community with others and in public or private, to manifest his religion or belief, in worship, teaching, practice and observance.

2. Freedom to manifest one's religion or beliefs shall be subject only to such limitations as are prescribed by law and are necessary in a democratic society in the interests of public safety, for the protection of public order, health or morals, or for the protection of the rights and freedoms of others.

Article 10
Freedom of expression

1. Everyone has the right to freedom of expression. This right shall include freedom to hold opinions and to receive and impart information and ideas without interference by public authority and regardless of frontiers. This article shall not prevent States from requiring the licensing of broadcasting, television or cinema enterprises.

2. The exercise of these freedoms, since it carries with it duties and responsibilities, may be subject to such formalities, conditions, restrictions or penalties as are prescribed by law and are necessary in a democratic society, in the interests of national security, territorial integrity or public safety, for the prevention of disorder or crime, for the protection of health or morals, for the protection of the reputation or rights of others, for preventing the disclosure of information received in confidence, or for maintaining the authority and impartiality of the judiciary.

Article 11
Freedom of assembly and association

1. Everyone has the right to freedom of peaceful assembly and to freedom of association with others, including the right to form and to join trade unions for the protection of his interests.

2. No restrictions shall be placed on the exercise of these rights other than such as are prescribed by law and are necessary in a democratic society in the interests of national security or public safety, for the prevention of disorder or crime, for the protection of health or morals or for the protection of the rights and freedoms of others. This article shall not prevent the imposition of lawful restrictions on the exercise of these rights by members of the armed forces, of the police or of the administration of the State.

Article 12
Right to marrry

Men and women of marriageable age have the right to marry and to found a family, according to the national laws governing the exercise of this right.

Article 14
Prohibition of discrimination

The enjoyment of the rights and freedoms set forth in this Convention shall be secured without discrimination on any ground such as sex, race, colour, language, religion, political or other opinion, national or social origin, association with a national minority, property, birth or other status.

Article 16
Restrictions on political activity of aliens

Nothing in Articles 10, 11 and 14 shall be regarded as preventing the High Contracting Parties from imposing restrictions on the political activity of aliens.

Article 17
Prohibition of abuse of rights

Nothing in this Convention may be interpreted as implying for any State, group or person any right to engage in any activity or perform any act aimed at the destruction of any of the rights and freedoms set forth herein or at their limitation to a greater extent than is provided for in the Convention.

Article 18
Limitations on use of restrictions on rights

The restrictions permitted under this Convention to the said rights and freedoms shall not be applied for any purpose other than those for which they have been prescribed.

The First Protocol
Article 1

Every natural or legal person is entitled to the peaceful enjoyment of his possessions. No one shall be deprived of his possessions except in the public interest and subject to the conditions provided for by law and by the general principles of international law.

The preceeding provisions shall not, however, in any way impair the right of a State to enforce such laws as it deems necessary to control the use of property in accordance with the general interest or to secure the payment of taxes or other contributions or penalties.

Article 2

No person shall be denied the right to education. In the exercise of any functions which it assumes in relation to education and to teaching, the State shall respect the right of parents to ensure such education and teaching in conformity with their own religious and philosophical convictions.

Article 3

The High Contracting Parties undertake to hold free elections at reasonable intervals by secret ballot, under conditions which will ensure the free expression of the opinion of the people in the choice of the legislature.

Index

Index of cases

Index of statutes